PEOPLE TYPES AND TIGER STRIPES
A Practical Guide to Learning Styles

Gordon Lawrence

University of Florida

CENTER FOR APPLICATIONS OF
PSYCHOLOGICAL TYPE, INC.

Published by Center for Applications of Psychological Type, Inc.
1441 N.W. 6th St. B-400, Gainesville, Fla. 32601

Library of Congress Cataloging in Publication Data

Lawrence, Gordon. 1930-
  People types and tiger stripes.

  1. Teaching.   2. Individualized instruction.
3. Study, Method of.   I.   Title.
LB1025.2.L38   371.1'02
Library of Congress Catalog Number 79-23413
ISBN 0 - 935652 - 01 - 9

To Isabel Myers and Mary McCaulley
who taught me about type theory,
and to my family—Cherie, Karen, and Mark—
who showed me how it works.

CONTENTS

INTRODUCTION

Lisa is a problem for her teachers. She's bright enough, but she seems to value popularity above everything else. Talkative, friendly and gregarious, she relies on her friends to make decisions for her and she patterns her behavior after theirs. Adults see her as flighty, unsure of her own preferences and point of view. Her work and conversations are often trite and shallow. Sometimes her classmates are annoyed by her "helpfulness;" they wish she would mind her own business. When criticized by a teacher or her friends, she seems deeply hurt and resentful.

Lisa frustrates her teachers not because she disrupts class or resists assignments. The problem is that they realize her personal development is not going well and they feel powerless to do anything about it. Perhaps, through their planning meetings, they can focus on a strategy to help Lisa develop some perspective and "a mind of her own." But at least 50 more of the students they see every day need attention as much as Lisa does. There is not time to work out a strategy for each of them.

Matching instruction to each student's uniqueness is, in most situations, an unrealizable objective. Yet to ignore individual differences in learners is foolish. Without straining to attend to uniqueness, it is possible to identify patterns in students that can serve as shortcuts to matching instruction to individuals. Consider Lisa's case, for example. Do you see in her a pattern you recognize? Probably every classroom has a "Lisa." The teacher who can recognize the basic ingredients in Lisa's behavior, who can see a motivation pattern, can then make an educated, shortcut prediction about what teaching strategy will work best with Lisa.

This book presents one way to identify learning styles and motivation patterns and it shows how to use the patterns in planning instruction. Behind the book lies a long, personal search the author has made to find practical and effective means of matching instruction to basic differences in students. A variety of approaches exists. Many of them merit attention. The approach presented here is based on Carl Jung's ideas about psychological types, as made practical through the work of Isabel Briggs Myers.[*] Theirs is a remarkable theory that offers a fresh perspective on people's patterns of dealing with their world.

---

[*]Jung, Carl G. **Psychological Types.** London: Rutledge & Kegan Paul, 1923; Myers, Isabel Briggs. **Gifts Differing.** Palo Alto: Consulting Psychologists Press, 1979.

This book includes readings and instructions for activities that explain the theory and guide you in making applications of it. The book may be used to guide a workshop or as a basis for group study; or it may be used by individuals. The activities that are designed for small groups can be accomplished by individuals with the occasional assistance of a colleague. The book is addressed specifically to teachers, but many other people in the helping professions should be able to translate the ideas and activities to their own professional framework.

CHAPTER ONE

PEOPLE TYPES AND TIGER STRIPES

People's habits tell a lot about them. Not just their "bad habits," but also such habits as what they pay attention to, what they care about, and how they decide things. These are mental habits.

Do you know any people with mental habits like these? Chris is quick to notice people's feelings, and tries to stay out of arguments. Jan likes to argue, likes to explain things, and doesn't notice people's feelings. John's father wants him to keep a careful record of how he spends his weekly allowance. John says record keeping isn't important to him. Pat wishes her mother would watch the clock more and get to places on time. Pat's mother wishes Pat would relax and not get an ulcer over being late five minutes.

Some mental habits are very deep in a person. Trying to change them is like trying to change the stripes on a tiger—like trying to change the grain in a piece of wood. The information that follows is about mental habits—the kind we probably can't change but can learn to use better.

The deep mental habits come in patterns, in combinations. Described below are eight patterns you can use to study yourself, your friends and family. Pick out your own patterns. There are no right or wrong patterns. Think carefully and try to pick the patterns that really describe you best.

1. Which pattern describes you better, **E** or **I**?

E	**I**
E likes action and variety	**I** likes quiet and time to consider things
E thinks best when talking with people	**I** likes to think things out before talking
E acts quickly, sometimes without thinking	**I** won't try something without understanding it first
E likes to get a job done, to see results, and to see how other people do it	**I** prefers jobs that can be worked on quietly, inside one's own head
E wants to know what others expect of him or her	**I** prefers to work alone or with few people and to set his or her own standards

E's interest turns mostly outward to the world of action, people and things. I's interest turns more often to the inner world of ideas and private things. Everyone turns outward to act and inward to reflect. You must do both, but you are more comfortable doing one or the other, just as right-handers are more comfortable with the right hand. Circle the **E** or the **I** in the margin to show which pattern fits you better.

E I

> **E** stands for extraversion, which means outward turning.
> **I** stands for introversion, which means inward turning.

2. Which pattern describes you better, **S** or **N**?

S	N
S pays most attention to the solid facts of experience	**N** likes to use imagination and look for hidden meanings in things
S likes to use eyes and ears and other senses to find out what's happening	**N** likes to think up new ways of doing things, new possibilities
S dislikes new problems unless there are standard ways to solve them	**N** likes solving new problems, dislikes doing the same thing over
S enjoys using skills already learned more than learning new ones	**N** enjoys learning new skills but may not use many of them
S is patient with details but impatient when the details get complicated	**N** is impatient with details but doesn't mind complicated situations

S pays most attention to the facts that come from personal experience. **S** can more easily see the details, while **N** can more easily see the "big picture." **N** pays most attention to meanings behind the facts.

S N   **S** and **N** are two kinds of perception, that is, two ways of finding out or giving attention to experiences. **S** stands for sensing and **N** stands for intuition. Everybody uses both their sensing and their intuition to find out things. You use both, but you use one more than the other. Circle the **S** or the **N** in the margin to show which pattern fits you better.

3. **T** and **F** are two ways of making judgments. Which pattern describes you better, **T** or **F**?

T	F
T likes to decide things logically	**F** likes to decide things with personal feelings and human values, even if they aren't logical
T wants to be treated with justice and fair play	**F** likes praise, and likes to please people, even in unimportant things

T sometimes ignores and hurts other peoples' feelings without knowing it	**F** is aware of other peoples' feelings
T gives more attention to ideas or things than in human relationships	**F** gets upset by arguments and conflicts; values harmony
T doesn't need harmony	**F** can predict how others will feel

T F **T** makes decisions by examining facts, staying impersonal and cool. **T** stands for thinking judgment. **F** makes decisions by paying attention to personal values and feelings. **F** stands for feeling judgment. You make **T** and **F** judgments every day, but you use one kind of judgment more than the other. Circle the **T** or the **F** in the margin to show which pattern fits you better.

4. The last two patterns have the letters **J** and **P**. Which pattern describes you better, **J** or **P**?

J	P
J likes to have a plan, to have things settled and decided ahead	**P** likes to stay flexible and avoid fixed plans
J tries to help make things to be "the way they ought to be"	**P** deals easily with unplanned and unexpected happenings
J's mind is usually made up	**P** starts too many projects and has trouble finishing them
J likes to finish one project before starting another	**P** would rather understand things than evaluate them
J may decide things too quickly	**P** may decide things too slowly
J wants to be right	**P** wants to miss nothing
J lives by standards and beliefs not easily changed	**P** is likely to put off unpleasant jobs

J P Circle the **J** or **P** in the margin to show which pattern fits you better. **J** stands for judgment and **P** stands for perception. **J** people use their thinking and feeling judgment more easily than they use their sensing and intuitive perception. The opposite is true for **P** people; they use perception more than judgment in dealing with the world outside themselves.

5. Now you can put together the four letters of the patterns that describe you best. Draw a circle here around the same letters you circled in the margins above.

  E   I   S   N   T   F   J   P

Now write your four letters here: ____ ____ ____ ____.
The four letters together tell you your "type."

There are 16 different "people types" as shown by the 16 combinations of the letters. Find yours.

ISTJ	ISFJ	INFJ	INTJ
ISTP	ISFP	INFP	INTP
ESTP	ESFP	ENFP	ENTP
ESTJ	ESFJ	ENFJ	ENTJ

Each type is different from the others in important ways. As you come to understand the type ideas better, you will see how type affects your life with your friends and family, at school or in a job.

The activity you have just completed is one you may want to use with students. With young students in mind, I wrote it in as simple language as I could. You may photocopy and reproduce the activity for students, giving credit to this publication.

The four dimensions of type (E I, S N, T F, and J P) and the ideas behind the sixteen types represent the lifelong work of Isabel Briggs Myers. In 1962 Educational Testing Service published the Myers-Briggs Type Indicator, a paper and pencil instrument she developed with Katharine Briggs over a twenty-year period. Regarded as a research instrument, it did not have wide circulation or usage until Consulting Psychologists Press assumed responsibility for publishing it in 1975. The Indicator was developed specifically to carry Carl Jung's theory of type (Jung, 1923) into practical applications.

The rest of this book will be more useful to you if you have taken the Indicator and are aware of your own profile. The Indicator was written to be taken by people who have not yet studied about type. Spontaneous responses probably give a more accurate profile, so the time to take the Indicator is before you proceed with this book. If you have not yet taken it, inquire about a local source that can administer it and give you information about your type. Persons qualified to order instruments from Consulting Psychologists Press may order the Indicator from them. The address is: 577 College Ave., Palo Alto, California 94306. Write for a price list. The question booklets are reusable. There are two means of scoring the responses: by handscoring keys that can be purchased from CPP, or by a computer scoring service that provides each person with a print-out of his/her type profile and an interpretation of it. The cost of the computer service is $4.00 each, with discounts for quantity. To obtain a price list and order form for computer scoring write: Center for Applications of Psychological Type, Inc., 1441 NW 6th Street, Suite B-400, Gainesville, Florida 32601.

CPP and CAPT also distribute *Introduction to Type* by Isabel Myers, a booklet that gives a basic explanation of type concepts. Because *Introduction to Type* is a necessary resource for interpreting your results from the Indicator, it has been reproduced in this book as an Appendix.

If your responses to the Indicator are scored by the computer service, your print-out will show your profile and a description of your type. If your response sheet is handscored, look up the description of your four-letter type in *Introduction to Type* (the Table of Contents on page A-1 will show you where to find your type description).

Look again at the type formula you chose while reading the "People Types and Tiger Stripes" activity. If it does not agree with the type derived from the Indicator, look it up in *Introduction to Type* and compare the two descriptions. Decide which one best matches you. Don't expect to understand type concepts quickly. Their meanings will present themselves to you at times and in circumstances that will surprise you. For now, read *Introduction to Type*, all 18 pages, with special attention to pages A2-A6.

Jung's Theory of Psychological Types°

The great Swiss physician-psychologist, C. G. Jung, developed one of the most comprehensive of current theories to explain human personality. Jung's theory of psychological types postulates that there are four basic mental processes (sensing, intuition, thinking and feeling), used by everyone, but not equally preferred and developed. Every type uses all four processes, but persons of each type are distinguished by their *relative* preferences for each of the four, and by the attitudes in which they use them.

In normal development, members of each type are motivated to use the processes they are disposed to prefer; through practice, they develop expertise in the activities for which their preferred processes are particularly useful. Skills and increased interests grow from "specializing" in preferred functions and lead to characteristic habits, attitudes and traits associated with the type. Types are not static but dynamic. In early life, the best development involves discovering one's natural predispositions and developing the preferred functions through meeting challenges with purposeful effort. Early life is a period of specialization, and failure to specialize was characterized by Jung as resulting in a primitive or undifferentiated personality. The theory allows for continued growth and development throughout life, as each type comes to greater appreciation of and command over functions which in early life were less interesting and less developed.

The dynamic and growing command of mental processes as an integral part of the theory is emphasized here, for two reasons. First, the word *type* connotes to many people a static rather than a dynamic system. A more

---

°McCaulley, M. H. **Application of the Myers-Briggs Type Indicator to Medicine and the Other Health Professions.** HRA Contract 231-76-0051, DHEW, January 1978.

5

important reason for stressing the developmental dynamics of the theory is that young people are, in theory, at a stage where they are still gaining command of perception and judgment.

Perceptive Functions: Sensing and Intuition

Sensing (S) is the term used for perception of the observable by way of the senses. **Intuition** (N) is the term used for perception of meanings, relationships and possibilities by way of insight. Sensing types (S) use sensing and intuition but prefer, and therefore develop sensing. With good type development, the expertise in sensing can lead to a differentiated awareness of present experience, acute powers of observation, a memory for facts and detail, and a capacity for realism, for seeing the world as it is. Attitudes characteristically developed as a preference for sensing include a reliance on experience rather than on theory, a trust of the conventional and customary way of doing things, a preference for beginning with what is known and real, and moving systematically and step-by-step, tying each new fact to past experience and testing it for its relevance in practical use. To most sensing types, "real intelligence" is characterized as being sound, accurate and having common sense.

Sensing types are attracted to careers and settings where skillful application of well-learned knowledge is more important than developing new solutions, where working with tangibles is more important than using theory and insight, and where dealing with the immediate situation using conventional wisdom is more important than making bold new breakthroughs.

Intuitive types (N) use sensing and intuition, but prefer and therefore develop intuition. With good type development, development of intuition can lead to insight into complexity, an ability to see abstract, symbolic and theoretical relationships, and a capacity to see future possibilities, often creative ones.

Attitudes characteristically developed as a result of a preference for intuition include a reliance on inspiration more than past experience, an interest in the new and untried, and a preference for learning new materials through an intuitive grasp of the meanings and relationships. To most intuitive types, "real" intelligence is shown by insight in grasping complexities, and flashes of creativity.

Intuitive types are attracted to careers and settings where finding the pattern in complex systems is more important than applying the details of well-learned knowledge, where creating new knowledge is more important than applying existing knowledge, where working with theory and insight is more important than dealing with tangibles, and where access to challenges for intellectual interests and new insights is more available than enjoyment of the pleasures of everyday events.

6

Judgment Functions: Thinking and Feeling

Thinking is the term used to define a logical decision-making process, aimed at an impersonal finding. **Feeling** is a term for a process of appreciation, making judgments in terms of a system of subjective, personal values. Both thinking and feeling are considered rational processes because they use reasoning to arrive at conclusions or decisions.

Thinking types (T) use both thinking and feeling but prefer to use thinking for making judgments. With good type development, expertise in thinking leads to powers of analysis and an ability to weight facts objectively including consequences, unintended as well as intended. Attitudes typically developed from a preference for thinking include objectivity, impartiality, a sense of fairness and justice, and skill in applying logical analysis. Thinking types are attracted to areas where tough-mindedness and technical skills are needed.

Feeling types (F) use thinking and feeling but prefer to reach judgments through feeling. With good type development, feeling leads to development of values and standards, and a knowledge of what matters most to themselves and other people. Attitudes typically resulting from a preference for feeling include an understanding of people and wish to affiliate with them, a desire for harmony, and a capacity for warmth, empathy and compassion. Feeling types are attracted to areas where understanding and communication with people is needed, and find the interpersonal skills more interesting than the technical skills.

Two Basic Orientations to Life: Extraversion and Introversion

Jung postulated two fundamentally different attitudes toward the world, which all humans share. In the *extraverted* attitude, attention flows out—is drawn out—to the objects and people of the environment. There is a desire to act on the environment, to affirm its importance and to increase it. In the *introverted* attitude, energy seems to flow from the object back to the subject; energy is abstracted from the environment and conserved by consolidating it within one's own position. The analogy has been made that extraverted energy penetrates the environment like radiant heating, while introverted energy is generated more like a heat pump.

Extraverts (E) go back and forth from extraverting to introverting, but prefer extraverting. With mature type development, extraverts typically create a life with action, social contacts, and a wide circle of acquaintance-ships. Characteristics typical of those who prefer the extraverted attitude are sociability, outspokenness, ease of communication, awareness of and reliance on the environment for stimulation and guidance, and an action-oriented, often impulsive way of meeting new events. Extraverts prefer activities requiring frequent interactions, quick action, and communication.

7

Introverts (I) are persons who go back and forth from introversion to extraversion, but who prefer and spend more time in the introverted attitude. Introverts typically create a life with time for contemplation, socializing with intimates and close friends. Characteristics typical of those who prefer the introverted attitude are a thoughtful contemplative detachment, interest in clear conceptualization of ideas, and a relative unawareness of changes in the outer situation, discounting their importance in any important decisions. Privacy and time to go into depth are important for introverts, who are postulated to have a greater capacity for sustained attention than extraverts. Introverts prefer activities requiring sustained attention, contemplation and specialties where relatively less communication is required.

Judging and Perceiving Attitudes

A fourth preference, **Judgment** (J) or **Perception** (P), is used in the Myers-Briggs Type Indicator to identify which of the two preferred processes is the dominant one.

Judging types (J) take both the perceptive and the judging attitudes, but prefer to deal with activities of the world around them mainly by means of their preferred judging process, thinking or feeling. A preference for the judging attitude leads to a desire for decisions, with a minimum of information-gathering. Judging types tend to prefer to organize and plan their lives, using their energies to control events more than in understanding them. When at their best, they are likely to be rated responsible, dependable and decisive.

Perceptive types (P) take both the perceptive and the judging attitudes, but prefer to deal with activities of the world around them by means of their preferred perceptive process, sensing or intuition. A preference for the perceptive attitude leads to an open, curious desire for understanding events with relatively little pressure to control them. When at their best, perceptive types are called receptive, understanding and flexible.

Opposites, Dominants, Auxiliaries and Shadows

Each type has characteristic strengths, weaknesses, and preferences. Examine the table on the following page. It contains a very brief characterization of the 16 types. Condensing the type descriptions into one table involves some oversimplification and distortion, so use it cautiously. Note that the types are arranged by opposites; e.g., ENTJ across from its opposite, ISFP. Opposites have the most difficulty communicating with each other; and, ironically, they stand to gain the most from trying to understand and use each other's strengths. Your opposite also describes what you do least well. It is the least developed side of you. Maturity in terms of type is the capability to use whatever process is needed when it is needed. Your opposite points out the direction in which you have the greatest room to grow.

8

BRIEF DESCRIPTIONS OF THE SIXTEEN TYPES

E N T J

Intuitive, innovative ORGANIZER; aggressive, analytic, systematic; more tuned to new ideas and possibilities than to people's feelings.

E S T J

Fact-minded, practical ORGAN-IZER; aggressive, analytic, systematic; more interested in getting the job done than in people's feelings.

I N T P

Inquisitive ANALYZER; reflective, independent, curious; more interested in organizing ideas than situations or people.

I S T P

Practical ANALYZER; values exactness; more interested in organizing data than situations or people; reflective, a cool and curious observer of life.

E S T P

REALISTIC ADAPTER in the world of material things; good natured, tolerant, easy going; oriented to practical, first hand experience; highly observant of details of things.

E S F P ·

REALISTIC ADAPTER in human relationships; friendly and easy with people, highly observant of their feelings and needs; oriented to practical, first hand experience.

I S T J

Analytical MANAGER OF FACTS AND DETAILS; dependable, decisive, painstaking and systematic; concerned with systems and organization; stable and conservative.

I S F J

Sympathetic MANAGER OF FACTS AND DETAILS; concerned with peoples' welfare; dependable, painstaking and systematic; stable and conservative.

I S F P

Observant, loyal HELPER; reflective, realistic, empathic; patient with details, gentle and retiring; shuns disagreements; enjoys the moment.

I N F P

Imaginative, independent HELPER; reflective, inquisitive, empathic, loyal to ideals; more interested in possibilities than practicalities.

E S F J

Practical HARMONIZER and worker-with-people; sociable, orderly, opinioned; conscientious, realistic and well tuned to the here and now.

E N F J

Imaginative HARMONIZER and worker-with-people; sociable, expressive, orderly, opinioned, conscientious; curious about new ideas and possibilities.

I N F J

People-oriented INNOVATOR of ideas; serious, quietly forceful and persevering; concerned with the common good, with helping others develop.

I N T J

Logical, critical, decisive INNO-VATOR of ideas; serious, intent, highly independent, concerned with organization, determined and often stubborn.

E N F P

Warmly enthusiastic PLANNER OF CHANGE; imaginative, individualistic; pursues inspiration with impulsive energy; seeks to understand and inspire others.

E N T P

Inventive, analytical PLANNER OF CHANGE; enthusiastic and independent; pursues inspiration with impulsive energy; seeks to understand and inspire others.

9

Note that two of the letters of each type formula are in bold type. The bold letters are very important for several reasons:

1. The E or the I being highlighted reminds us of the type's **orientation** to life, outward for action or inward for reflection.

2. They show the **dominant** process of each type—one of the four middle letters: S, N, T or F. For example, the **ISFP**'s dominant process is F. The process opposite the dominant one is the **shadow,** the least available and least used process. For example, the **ISFP**'s shadow is T.

3. The bold letters remind us that introverted people use their dominant process mainly in their inner world, their more important world, while extroverted people use their dominant process in the outer world where people see it. The **ENTJ**, for example, readily shows the thinking process, the dominant process; but the **ISFP**, in whom feeling is dominant, shows not the dominant/favorite process (F), but the **auxiliary** process (S), the second strongest process. So **ISFP**'s and **INFP**'s, the introverted feeling types, keep the feeling side inside. Note that the two other introversion-feeling combinations, **ISFJ** and **INFJ**, have feeling as the auxiliary process, so they show their feeling judgments more.

Talk About Type Concepts

I have explained the Myers Briggs Type Indicator and type concepts to many teachers. Nearly all of them have benefitted from talking about the concepts with colleagues, family and friends. You are likely to get the most out of this book if you are part of a group of four or five colleagues using the book together. This is a good point to begin your discussions, if you have not started talking already. Convene a meeting. Each person should bring to the meeting: MBTI profile and this book. In addition the group will need several apples, at least one for each person. Here are some suggestions for the agenda of your meeting. Keep your own notes for possible further use.

A. Share reactions to your MBTI profiles. If you know each other well, you may want to guess each other's type formula.

B. The object of this meeting is to help each other understand the concepts of "people types." Raise questions you have about the concepts. Your group may want to review specific portions of *Introduction to Type.*

C. Discuss opposites, dominants, auxiliaries and shadows, using the "Brief Descriptions of the Sixteen Types."

D. Now you can stop wondering what the apples are for. They are to help you get a deeper insight into the four mental processes: sensing, intuition, thinking and feeling. Follow the activity instructions, "Eat An Apple."

EAT AN APPLE*

A. This activity is to help you distinguish the mental processes of perception (intuiting and sensing) and judgment (thinking and feeling). Work in pairs with one partner being a recorder. The recorder should mark off four sections on a sheet of note paper. Label one section Sensing, one Intuition, one Feeling, and one Thinking. As both partners talk, the recorder should make notes in each section, as indicated below, starting with sensing. Each person select and eat an apple, paying attention to each of the four processes separately, one at a time. Take three or four minutes for each process.

1) As you eat the apple, list your sense impressions of the apple and its parts: skin, flesh, carpels, seeds—noting colors, shapes, textures, tastes, muscular movements and tensions. List facts only.

2) List your intuitions that come to you during the experience. Memories and associations: Who or what do apples make you think of? Can you recall other ways of enjoying apples? baked? jellies or ciders? games? other? Do you recall apples in stories, myths, poems, proverbs, or superstitions? Do you find yourself speculating about this particular apple?

3) List your feeling judgments:
How you felt about trying this experiment.
How you felt about selecting the particular apple you did.
How you felt about eating the apple you chose.

4) Can you think about apples?
Did your sense impressions or your intuitions lead you to make any logical conclusions about this apple? About apples in general? "I'd say this apple has been in cold storage. I say that because . . ."

B. Each recorder read to the others in the group what was written in the sensing section. Get concurrence that all items were sensory data. Then read each of the other three similarly.

*Adapted from Anna Nuernberger and Gordon Lawrence, **Personality Influences in Teaching and Learning,** Florida Modules on Generic Teaching Competencies. Tallahassee: Florida Department of Education, 1973. By permission. The idea for the activity was suggested by Alan Bundick.

11

C. The group then discuss this question: In what ways is the set of data recorded under "sensing" fundamentally different from the kinds of things listed under "intuition?" Do all members of the group agree? Do the two sets of data help to show why people who perceive with their senses more than with their intuition, and who dwell more on sensory data than intuitive data, are fundamentally different from intuitive types (and vice versa)? Can you see why they would be more tuned to concrete facts, in the "here and now," and less tuned in to abstractions, imaginings, possibilities and speculations? Now consider the notes under "feeling" and "thinking." How are these two kinds of judgment statements basically different? Do they help to show the real differences between **F** types and **T** types?

Check Your Knowledge of Type Concepts

Before going on to applications of type to educational settings, you may wish to see how well you grasp the concepts. Here is a word list you can use to review the ideas. Following that is a Type Concepts Test and an answer key with which you may check your responses. To make a practical check of your understanding, try one or both of these activities:

1. Find several people (colleagues, family, students, etc.) who are interested in taking the Myers-Briggs Type Indicator. Arrange to have them take it, explain the theory to them, and, if appropriate, have them check their comprehension with the Type Concepts Test. (This activity is less cumbersome than it sounds. Typically, people who learn about the MBTI want to talk with someone about it; and this activity encourages you to talk about it with care and thereby test your comprehension of the theory.)

2. Select a professional colleague to be a partner, one whose type is different from yours. Arrange to observe each other informally in several different situations, and discuss with each other the ways that type shows up in everyday behavior. You will want to use the booklet *Introduction to Type* for ideas of what to observe and as a resource in developing your capacities to observe each other.

Words to Help Understanding of Type Concepts

Sensing

Perceiving with the five senses
Practical and factual
Fun loving
In touch with reality
Interest in what is going on in the present
Confining attention to what is said and done

12

Appreciating "little things" of everyday life
"Hard-headed realist"
"The eyes tell the mind . . ."

Intuition

Perceiving with memory and associations
Seeing meanings
Having hunches
Seeing possibilities
Imagining
Interest in possibilities for the future
"Ideas out of nowhere"
"Reading between the lines"
"The mind tells the eyes . . . ."

Thinking Judgment

Logical
Skeptical
Impersonal reasoning
Deductive
Firm
Cause and effect analysis

Feeling Judgment

Personal priorities
Human values and motives
Appreciation
Warmth
Prizing harmony
Trusting

Extraversion

Living more in the outer world
Preferring to focus on people and things
Active
Using trial and error with confidence
Using the dominant process in dealing with others
Using the auxiliary process in the inner (introverted) life

Introversion

Living more in the inner world
Preferring to focus on ideas and concepts

Reflective
Wanting to consider deeply before acting
Using the dominant process in the inner world
Using the auxiliary process in dealing with others

Judging

Deciding and planning
Organizing and scheduling
Controlling and regulating
Using feeling or thinking judgment
Goal oriented
"The evidence is in. Let's act."

Perceiving

Taking in information
Adapting and changing
Understanding
Open-minded
Spontaneous and flexible
"There's more to it than that."

Dominant Process

Favorite among S, N, T or F
Governing force
Unifies one's life
Best developed and most used process
"The ship's captain"

Auxiliary Process

Second favorite among S, N, T or F
A perceptive (S or N) process if the dominant is judgment (T or F)
A judging (T or F) process if the dominant is perception (S or N)
Used in the outer world if the dominant is introverted
Used in the inner world if the dominant is extraverted
"The ship's navigator"

The Shadow

The opposite of the dominant (as S is opposite N, T is opposite F)
The least developed process
Our relatively childish and primitive perception or judgment
An escape from the conscious personality
Is in charge when "You don't act yourself"

TYPE CONCEPTS TEST*

Record your multiple-choice responses on a separate sheet and check your answers with the key which immediately follows the test. Some of the items have more than one correct answer.

1. Type theory is concerned with the valuable differences in personality that result from the way people
   a. think and feel
   b. use their sensing and intuition
   c. perceive and judge

2. The term "dominant process" in type theory means
   a. either extraversion or introversion
   b. either judgment or perception
   c. the favorite process, the one used most

3. The auxiliary process is
   a. the opposite of the dominant
   b. either thinking or feeling
   c. the second favorite

4. If the favorite process is a judging one, the second favorite is
   a. also a judging one
   b. a perceptive one
   c. any of the other processes

5. If the second favorite process is a judging one, the favorite will be
   a. a perceptive one
   b. also a judging one
   c. any of the other processes

6. By extravert is meant
   a. a gregarious type who talks a lot
   b. a shallow person
   c. one who prefers to focus on people and things

7. By introvert is meant
   a. one who prefers to focus on ideas and concepts
   b. one who is aloof and unsociable
   c. a neurotic

---

*From Anna Nuernberger and Gordon Lawrence, **Personality Influences in Teaching and Learning.** By Permission.

8. By sensing type is meant
   a. one who is sensitive and empathetic
   b. one who is sensuous
   c. one who prefers to perceive through the five senses

9. By intuitive is meant
   a. one who has prophetic powers
   b. one who values imagination, inspirations, and possibilities
   c. one who has extrasensory perception

10. By thinking judgment is meant making judgments
    a. by means of all the mental processes
    b. logically and impersonally
    c. taking into account all the data

11. By feeling judgment is meant
    a. immature, emotional judgments
    b. irrational and illogical judgments
    c. judging on the basis of human motives and values

12. One's orientation to life is either
    a. judgment or perception
    b. extraversion or introversion
    c. the dominant or the auxiliary process

13. One's attitude toward the outer world is
    a. either judging or perceptive
    b. governed by the favorite process
    c. governed by the second favorite process

14. The effects of the combinations of perception and judgment
    a. are arbitrary and unpredictable
    b. produce the different types of personalities
    c. produce different sets of interests, values, needs, habits of mind and surface traits

15. Sensing plus thinking people are mainly interested in
    a. facts, which can be collected and verified by the senses
    b. possibilities which reveal themselves in new data and experiences
    c. problems which allow them to use their ingenuity

16. Sensing plus feeling people are mainly interested in
    a. the impersonal and logical handling of other people
    b. making decisions about facts which take into account how people feel
    c. problems which allow them to use their imagination

17. The intuition plus feeling people are
    a. most interested in projects they have completed themselves
    b. most interested in possibilities for people
    c. are interested in the facts relevant to all projects

18. The intuition plus thinking people
    a. are fact oriented, and skillful in handling people
    b. are interested in possibilities which they approach with impersonal analysis
    c. choose projects which do not require executive or technical ability

19. The last letter in the type formula indicates the attitude you take toward the outer world
    a. if you are an extravert
    b. if you are an introvert
    c. for both introverts and extraverts

20. The introverts rely on their auxiliary process
    a. for dealing with the outer world
    b. for dealing with the inner world of ideas
    c. in the same way as the extravert

21. The introverted judging types (with a J in their type formula) have as their favorite process
    a. a judging process, either thinking or feeling
    b. a perceptive process, either intuition or sensing
    c. any of the four mental processes named above

22. The extraverted judging types (with a J in their type formula) have as their favorite process
    a. a judging process, either thinking or feeling
    b. a perceptive process, either intuition or sensing
    c. any of the four mental processes named above

23. The three questions above reflect
    a. some of the basic differences between introverts and extraverts
    b. why introverts seem so complex and difficult to understand
    c. why a usually perceptive introvert may suddenly (and briefly) turn judging, and vice versa

24. The well-developed auxiliary process is necessary
    a. to prevent superficiality in the introvert
    b. to help the extravert put his or her best foot forward
    c. to help both extravert and introvert achieve balance, and keep them from ignoring either world

25. In types whose favorite process is a judging one, the perceptive auxiliary provides
    a. help in making quick decisions
    b. the raw material needed as a basis for judgment
    c. a second line of attack when the favorite process does not work

26. In types whose favorite process is a perceiving one, the judging auxiliary provides
    a. a steadiness of purpose
    b. a means of evaluating the worth of their perceptions and the uses to be made of them
    c. help in suspending judgment when data are insufficient

27. The remaining processes, after taking into account the dominant and auxiliary
    a. should be suppressed
    b. are not necessary, and can be ignored
    c. can make contributions toward greater effectiveness

28. A high score (over 20) on a dimension of the MBTI means
    a. a well-developed process
    b. a definite preference
    c. neglect of the opposite process

29. A low score (under 10) on a dimension of the MBTI means
    a. a less well developed process
    b. little preference between the choices
    c. that both processes may be developed almost equally well

30. The "tendencies" of the types
    a. are the way people are and nothing can be done about it
    b. are the talents you can aspire to realize, and the warnings of what to guard against
    c. are one of the most useful learnings one can experience from understanding type theory

31. Certain types
    a. will have trouble with other types
    b. can be of more use to you than other types
    c. will be easier to understand than other types

32. In conflicts, you can use your understanding of type
    a. by being sensitive to the other person's type
    b. by being certain that the other person is aware of your point of view
    c. to understand what it is that one of you sees and values more highly than the other

33. In education, you can use your understanding of type
    a. to plan more effective learning situations according to type
    b. by expecting a person to focus on processes intrinsically comfortable to him
    c. to plan situations which exercise all the processes and give children broad choices in developing their own type

ANSWERS TO THE TYPE CONCEPTS TEST

1. c. perceive and judge

   Thinking and feeling are the judging processes, intuition and sensing are the perceiving processes.

2. c. the favorite process, the one used most

   Extraversion or introversion is the orientation to life. Judging or perception is a global attitude rather than a process. Sensing, intuition, feeling and thinking are functions or processes, one of which will be dominant.

3. c. the second favorite

   The opposite of the dominant process conflicts with it, and is therefore the least developed of the four processes. The auxiliary, to be helpful, must serve the dominant process, not compete with it.

4. b. a perceptive one

   Its responsibility is to supply facts and understanding as a basis for judgment.

5. a. a perceptive one

   When the second favorite process (auxiliary) is a judging one, it is because the favorite (dominant) process is perceptive and needs a **judging** assistant.

6. c. one who prefers to focus on people and things

   Either of the other answers may reveal a prejudice you need to look at. Introverts may see extraverts as shallow because they have no way of knowing how satisfying the company of other people can be to an extravert.

7. a. one who prefers to focus on ideas and concepts

   If you chose either of the other answers, either you do not understand the meaning of the word introvert, or you have a prejudice which can affect your dealings with others. If you are an introvert yourself, you may lack the allegiance to your own type which is necessary for an effective and happy personality.

8. c. one who prefers to perceive through the five senses

   Being a sensing type brings with it no assurance that one will be either sensitive, empathetic or sensuous.

9. b. one who values imagination, inspirations and possibilities

10. b.   logically and impersonally

Thinking is often used to mean all the mental processes, but here we use it in a special way.

11. c.   judging on the basis of human motives and values

Mature people use their feeling judgment in a rational way. Emotion is the visible aspect of affect. A feeling judgment is one that weighs more heavily the human motives, feelings and values than impersonal logic.

12. b.   extraversion or introversion

This is called the orientation to life because extraversion means "to be focused outwardly," and introversion is "to be focused inwardly."

13. a.   judging or perceptive

The extravert's attitude toward the outer world is governed by the favorite process. The introvert's attitude toward the outer world is governed by the second favorite.

14. c.   produce different sets of interests, values, needs, habits of mind and surface traits

These are highly predictable in the types, which are the results of the combinations of the orientation (EI preference), the dominant and auxiliary processes, and the attitude toward the outer world (JP preferences).

15. a.   facts, which can be collected and verified by the senses.

16. b.   making decisions about facts which take into account how people feel

17. b.   most interested in possibilities for people.

18. b.   are interested in possibilities which they approach with impersonal analysis

19. c.   for both introverts and extraverts

20. a.   for dealing with the outer world

Introverts use their favorite process in their inner world, and consequently their "best side" is not seen by the casual observer, who only witnesses the less developed auxiliary (second favorite process). Extraverts, on the other hand, use their favorite process in the outer world, and the observer sees the best side of them at once.

21. b.   a perceptive process, either intuition or sensing
Conversely, the introverted perceptive types (with a P in their type formula, indicating the perceptive attitude toward the outer world) have as their favorite process a judging process, either thinking or feeling.

22. a.   a judging process, either thinking or feeling
Conversely, the extraverted perceptive types (with a P in their type formula) have as their favorite process a perceptive process, either intuition or sensing.

23. a.   some of the basic differences between introverts and extraverts
b.   why introverts seem so complex and difficult to understand
c.   why a usually perceptive introvert may suddenly (and briefly) turn judging and vice versa.
An introvert's introverted favorite process does not **always** stay introverted. On the rare occasions when an external matter is important enough, the "dominant process" does dominate outwardly, and everybody is surprised.

24. c.   to help both extravert and introvert to achieve balance, and keep them from ignoring either world
A well-developed auxiliary is necessary to help the introvert to be effective in the outer world and the extravert to be effective with ideas.

25. b.   the raw material needed as a basis for judgment
When the favorite process is a judging one, perceptions provide the information on which to make choices, and sound decisions are made only with adequate data.

26. a.   a steadiness of purpose
b.   a means of evaluating the worth of their perceptions and the uses to be made of these
Both answers are correct. Perceptive types with insufficient judgment may focus entirely on enjoying their perceptions, and make no further use of them.

27. c.   can make contributions toward greater effectiveness
The less developed processes must be heard. If they are suppressed too much, they will express themselves in embarrassing and detrimental ways. **All** the mental processes are used by everyone, and are necessary.

28. b.   a definite preference

A high score does not necessarily mean that the preferred process is well developed, nor that the opposite process is neglected.

29. a. or b. or c. may be correct

In younger subjects, the low score is more likely to indicate that neither process is clearly preferred and that they have not decided which to trust. In older subjects there is more chance than with younger ones that appropriate use is being made of both processes.

30. b.   are the talents you can aspire to realize, and the warnings of what to guard against

c.   are one of the most useful learnings one can experience from understanding type theory

a.   is correct to the extent that we should recognize that the preferred processes are those which are the most comfortable, and effectiveness depends on being able to function in the preferred ways.

31. b.   can be of more use to you than other types, and

c.   will be easier to understand than other types

Generally people who are very much alike have little trouble in agreeing about what should be done, but since they both have the same abilities and deficits, they will be of less help to one another than to people of slightly different types. People who are of very different types will see things very differently, and may have trouble getting along, but can be of great help to one another if they learn how to communicate with their opposite types.

32. a., b., and c. are correct

Once differences are identified and understood they can be discussed rather than fought over.

33. a., b., and c, are correct

Although all of us use all the processes, exercise both perception and judgment, and experience, in varying degrees, both the outer and the inner worlds, we learn best when we can learn according to our chosen type.

CHAPTER TWO

USING TYPE CONCEPTS IN PLANNING INSTRUCTION

Introduction

Schools across the United States, urban and rural, big and small, report that students' lack of motivation for school tasks is one of the most persistent and perplexing problems. Student motivation is, of course, very complex, having its roots in family life, peer relationships and societal pressures that lie beyond the teacher's range of influence. But teachers do have the power to affect student motivation in some respects; and one key to that power can be seen in the type concepts.

Type theory suggests that we break down motivation into four parts, corresponding to the four dimensions of type:

1. The extraversion-introversion preference shows the broad areas of a student's **natural interest**
2. The sensing-intuition preference reveals basic **learning style** differences
3. The thinking-feeling dimension shows patterns of **commitments and values** of a student
4. The judging-perceiving dimension shows **work habits.**

By taking these four natural motivators into account in planning instruction, by working with them rather than against them, the teacher can better direct student energies toward learning. This chapter shows how type concepts can be used for that purpose.

Two facts about type and classrooms

The 16 types are not evenly distributed in the school population. It is estimated that type in the general American population, and in most school populations, is distributed as follows:

Extraversion—70%--Introversion - 30%
Sensing—70%--Intuition - 30%
Thinking (female)—40%--Feeling (female) - 60%
Thinking (male)—60%--Feeling (male) - 40%
Judging—50%--Perceiving - 50%°

°These, and other statistics presented in the chapter, are from Isabel Myers, **Manual:** Myers-Briggs Type Indicator. Palo Alto: Consulting Psychologists Press, 1975.

This means many more students are ESFJ, for example, than are INFJ, and more are ENFJ than INFJ. The uneven distribution of the first two type dimensions, E I and S N, is a crucial fact for teachers, as can be seen in the diagram below. A typical classroom of 35 students would have this distribution of types:

I S 7	I N 3
E S 18	E N 7

(The distribution might be different for elective courses because students' type preferences often influence their choices of electives.)

If a classroom has six times as many ES___ types as IN___ types, what does that mean to the teacher? The question brings us to the second key fact: most school instruction gives an advantage to some types and handicaps others. Consider these three descriptions; do you regard them as typical of school instruction patterns?

1. Students work individually on their own tasks, each with his/her own set of materials or books. Quiet is expected so each one can concentrate and think through the work individually.
2. When new concepts or rules are introduced, the teacher (or textbook) tries to follow a sequence of first presenting the concept verbally, defining it; then giving examples, illustrations and/or demonstrations; and finally (at least sometimes) giving students an opportunity to use the concept or rule.
3. The main medium of instruction is words, spoken or written symbols. A student's successful manipulation of words in dialogue or on tests is the primary way that teachers have of judging a student's achievement. In the case of mathematics and some science knowledge, the symbols of instruction are abstractions representing things other than words.

Are the three descriptions typical? Yes, so much that they seem to be essential. Yet they clearly favor certain types of students. The first one is a natural format for introverts, who prefer to do most of their work quietly inside their own heads. Extraverts, 70% of the students, really do their best thinking with their mouths open. Extraverts want to push a half-formed idea out where others can react to it because the outer world of people and things is the one they value most. The most natural setting for extraverts, the one in which they learn best, is one that allows them to think out loud and to **act**—that is, to do, make, move, produce—rather than to use words **about** such actions. The testing of ideas and skills in the outer world tells the extravert whether the half-formed ideas and skills are worth having. The introvert, on the other hand, prefers to test ideas against private criteria, in the inner world of the mind—a process which is much easier for schools to manage.

The second classroom practice described above, that of presenting abstractions first and applications after, appeals to the intuitive's learning style, not to the sensing type. Abstractions, such as definitions, theories, lists of procedures and rules, help intuitive types get into a topic because they want to see the abstract meaning, the relationships to prior knowledge, the "big picture," before they take on new concrete experience.

A conversation that I had with a student at a diesel mechanics school will illustrate the point. The student was complaining about paper and pencil tests, saying he did much better with "hands-on" tests in the shop. "I think better with my hands." When asked to give an example, he told of being given a defective alternator he was to take apart, fix and reassemble. He was given a diagram to guide him in the operation. "I studied the diagram and studied it until I thought I would puke. I couldn't understand it. So I threw it down and figured out my own system of working on the alternator and found the trouble. It worked perfectly." Did he look at the diagram afterward? "Yes." Did he understand it then? "Yes, sure. It made sense then." To this sensing type student, the abstract diagram made sense as a map of the complex territory only **after** he first put his senses to work in understanding the territory. It seems likely that similar diagrams he encounters in the future will be more useful to him.

Probably the young man was an ES____ type. His best learning came when he could use a combination of senses, actively operating on the realities of his tangible environment. Note that he did not follow the prescribed sequence of instruction, beginning with the abstraction, the diagram.

How extensively are standard instruction practices biased toward introversion and intuition? No careful analysis has been made, but the bias is widespread. Probably the young child first encounters it in the teaching of reading. Of course, reading is primarily an introverted activity; it is done quietly by oneself. And it is fundamentally an intuitive activity, involving abstractions—the printed symbols. But reading need not be taught as if all students were introverts and intuitives. The skills of reading can be and are mastered by students of all types, and they all can leave school with a positive attitude toward reading. Tragically many students are alienated by their first encounters with reading instruction. Type theory points to the probability that most of the alienated children are extraverted sensing types. There are data which indicate that the dropout rate is much higher

26

among sensing children. Isabel Myers obtained type data from 500 people who did not finish 8th grade; 99% of them were sensing types.

What setting for reading instruction appeals to ES____ types? They learn best through action and many chances to talk: reading aloud with a partner; first experiencing something concrete that is worth reporting to someone not present, then dictating it and seeing it transcribed as a valuable record of experience; not memorizing "sight words" which may remain nonsense syllables, but learning to decode printed language through phonics, word attack skills.

Correcting the biases of instruction that harm ES____ type children is perhaps the most crucial unrecognized problem of American education. No doubt the biases are largely unconscious, unintended. But most textbook writers are intuitives, as are the writers of standardized tests. Most are probably unaware that their products reflect their **own** intuitive way of viewing the world, their way of approaching learning tasks. Writers of pencil and paper intelligence tests, also intuitives, most likely are unaware that their tests have a bias toward the kind of intelligence they value most, intuitive intelligence (manipulating symbols, drawing inferences, and the like). Considering the biases, there is no surprise in the fact that IN____ students as a group score highest on intelligence tests, followed by EN____, IS____ and ES____, in that order. The record of American education in the twentieth century is a record of neglect of sensing intelligence, an intelligence typified by the young diesel mechanics student who bypassed the prescribed instruction process and solved his problem his way . . . and the kind of intelligence possessed by the majority of American students.

Planning Instruction to Honor the Rights of Every Type

Certainly every student has a right to a learning setting that will offer him/her the best opportunity to develop. Type theory provides new insights into how to match learning settings to students.

The four checklists that follow represent one way of beginning the matching process. Use them first to identify your own most preferred and least preferred work or learning settings. Follow the directions. You may want to mark the items lightly in pencil so you can erase the marks later and use the pages as masters to photocopy for students' use.

I AM LIKELY TO DO MY BEST WORK . . .

DIRECTIONS: Put a check beside those items that are true for you, on all four lists. When you have finished that, go back over the four lists and draw a circle around the checkmark of items that are strongly true for you.

A PATTERN

I AM LIKELY TO DO MY BEST WORK IN SITUATIONS THAT:

—will produce practical results, useful products
—involve other people, group effort
—have goals set in advance and let me work toward them in an orderly way
—are real and not just dealing with theory
—give me a clear picture of what other people are doing and what they regard as important
—have realistic schedules that don't expect too much too soon
—let me learn from first-hand experience, on the job
—let me use the practical skills and facts I possess
—give me a regular work schedule, but give me some variety and time to socialize, too
—let me work with concrete things, hands-on materials
—let me "think out loud" with other people

B PATTERN

I AM LIKELY TO DO MY BEST WORK IN SITUATIONS THAT:

—make practical sense to me
—have a clear organization in them
—are practical and realistic
—let me know just what is expected of me
—let me work at a steady speed, step-by-step
—require accuracy and careful attention to details
—require patience
—don't have many surprises in them
—let me use my practical experience
—let me use my memory for facts
—let me think through a problem by myself before I have to act on it

---

C PATTERN

I AM LIKELY TO DO MY BEST WORK IN SITUATIONS THAT:

—put me on my own initiative
—let me plan and carry out new projects
—involve other people in solving problems, such as group projects
—let me create new ways of doing things
—let me try out my ideas to see if they work, to see how other people react to them
—don't require a detailed accounting of how I use my time
—pose problems needing more attention to the broad picture than to details
—provide variety and minimize routine
—let me figure out how to put theory into practice
—let me make mistakes without penalties and learn from the mistakes
—challenge my imagination

D PATTERN

I AM LIKELY TO DO MY BEST WORK IN SITUATIONS THAT:

—let me work in my head with my own ideas
—let me work toward solutions in my own way
—give me a chance to be creative
—let me set my own standards of quality
—let me work hard when I feel like it, and go easy when I need to
—don't burden me with too many routines
—have important ideas behind them
—give me ample time to think out my ideas before I have to act
—let me use my hunches and inspirations
—let me follow my curiosity
—let me work in depth on things of importance to me

Look back over your responses and see what patterns you find. As you may have discovered, the **A** list describes ES____ preferences for work situations, the **B** list IS____, the **C** list EN____, and the **D** list IN____. You probably put the most checkmarks on the list that matches your type, and the most circled checkmarks on that list. Very likely you also put the least checkmarks on the list opposite your type, as ES is opposite IN, and IS is opposite EN.

Now answer three questions, to your own satisfaction:
1. Does the list I marked most often really reflect work conditions that are highly important to me?
2. Would I probably work less productively under the other three sets of conditions?
3. Do the four lists apply as appropriately to schoolwork situations as to other kinds of work situations?

Most people answer yes to all three questions, including young people. Some adults spread checkmarks across two or three of the lists. Their maturity gives them the flexibility to work well in a variety of situations. Young people may be less adaptable, more polarized toward one pattern. For such students, the school's attention to matching of schoolwork situations to students' types becomes more urgent.

If the 16 types are distributed in your classroom as they are in the general population, you may expect a majority of your students to choose list A, with less choosing B and C, and very few choosing D.

The four lists were written to apply to any work situation, not just the classroom. They do not refer to "learning situations" or "learning style" because those terms call to mind the usual features of the classroom (lecture, workbooks, audio-visual materials, etc.), and those features make it difficult to look more broadly at learning situations. (Later in this chapter is a list of classroom features that different types prefer.)

You may find it helpful to go back through the four lists and respond to each item as if it were a question beginning thus: "In my teaching, do I typically provide learning situations that . . ." Be critical and mark only the items that describe what you regularly have provided for students. From this analysis you can identify what you most need to develop.

The following paragraphs describe a procedure for planning instruction that begins with the four lists you have analyzed. When thinking about instruction plans, keeping 16 models in mind is difficult if not impossible. A good place to begin is with four basic models: IS, IN, ES, and EN, as represented in the four lists you have just used. This approach does not abandon the T F and J P dimensions. Rather, it uses them as ways of making adjustments in the four basic models, adjustments to fit the needs of individual students, or of small groups.

30

Described on the following pages are three steps you may wish to follow in planning instruction with the help of type concepts:

1. Begin by planning for ES students' needs, the types most often neglected in instructional plans. This is your central plan. Check your plan by using the items of the ES list as criteria.
2. Develop alternative activities, variations from your central plan, that will appeal to IS, EN, and IN students.
3. Adjust the plans for T F and J P differences that you know will be important to individuals in the class.

Examples of Classroom Plans Successful with ES Students

Here are three examples of instructional plans that had a strong measure of concrete activity in them, that followed the three-step planning process, and were (predictably) successful with ES students as well as the others. Note that the teachers who planned and conducted these activities did not consciously follow the three-step plan, but in retrospect all the features of the planning process can be seen.

1. Sixth grade students in Jacksonville, Florida, became interested in the processes of plant growth and got the idea of building a greenhouse so they could house the number of plants they wanted to grow, and could continue growing them throughout the winter. Concrete activity was at the center of the plan: presenting the idea to the principal, a field trip to a local greenhouse, letter writing to obtain information about greenhouse construction, dialogues with a nurseryman, a businessman and a construction foreman (a parent), and maintaining a bulletin board related to the progress of the project.

Science and math work became concrete and active, too. Students made charts and graphs for the plant experiments; plotted the sun's movement in relation to the school to help decide the best location for the greenhouse; made careful measurements and worked up plans concerning the size, shape, materials and cost of the greenhouse; and the plant experiments themselves had many active aspects. All the students wanted to be involved in some way in the actual construction work: using the posthole diggers, sawing, hammering, and stapling the plastic covering on.

In analyzing the events as they evolved, we can see that ES and EN students would be equally drawn to the active aspects of the projects. Virtually all parts of the project were performed by teams, with the more quiet and reflective activities coordinated with the active work. The library research on greenhouses and the sun's path, and design work would appeal to IN's, as would the plant experiments themselves. IS's would be especially attracted to the planning work, learning from experienced adults, keeping accounts for the fund raising and calculating materials needed and the cost of them. Probably the IS students were also the most reliable in caring for the plants and recording outcomes.

The third step in the three-step planning process is to adjust instruction for the T F and J P needs of students. That procedure is described later in the chapter. The greenhouse project involves such varied activities that the teacher would have many options for accommodating the T F and J P needs of students.

2. Some Nashville junior high social studies teachers planned a very successful unit for students of their inner-city school. Many of the students had the ability to do well in school but most were expected to drop out because of what was termed their "defeatist" attitude. Most of the students lived in apartment buildings that were poorly maintained. No one knew the landlord; rent checks went to a realty company, and requests about repairs mostly went unheeded.

When the teachers learned about the housing conditions, they proposed a project for the students to find out more about the situation and to try to do something about it. Students agreed, without much enthusiasm at first. Investigative teams were formed. After preliminary planning, some teams took a questionnaire, a note pad and a camera to an apartment building to interview tenants and document the need for repairs. These teams kept records of how much rent was paid, what requests for repairs were made, when, and which were honored; and what repairs were still needed. Another team went to City Hall to find deeds and other documents that would show who the absentee landlords were.

After a file of facts, figures and photographs was prepared for each building, the students made an appointment with the landlord and presented him with the file. In two instances the file showed a very wide gap between the landlord's probable net return on his investment and the amount spent for maintenance and improvements. In several buildings, the students' project resulted in repairs and had other positive spinoffs. Some students and their families became active in tenant cooperatives and earned wages or rent rebates helping to care for their building.

Besides learning something about economics and local politics, the students more importantly gained a sense of their own capability to influence "the system" they had thought to be mysterious and inaccessible.

As with the greenhouse project, the central events of this unit were active and concrete, and were sufficiently varied that all of the 16 types would find activities of high interest to them.

3. Three middle school science teachers had planned a year's theme of human ecology. One activity, suggested by students, proved to be especially rewarding: collecting aluminum cans to be recycled. It not only led them into the issues of finite resources and recycling, but the income from the sale of the cans paid for the cost of bussing them on several field trips:

to a plant making aluminum extrusions, to a power plant to see how electricity is generated, to a small company that built solar heating units, to a sewage treatment facility and to a bird sanctuary. Among other things, students figured out techniques for saving energy at home and monitored their family's consumption of energy by charting the relative effect of various conservation measures. As they became aware of ecological problems in their community, the students also wrote letters to the editor of the newspaper and a group of them presented a proposal to the city council.

These activities were the more dramatic highlights of a year of study, and they were strong motivating elements for the more typical activities: use of textbooks, films, resource persons, library report work and some laboratory experiments.

The thread common to the three examples of instructional planning is the emphasis on active and concrete experience being the center of attention of students. Other activities, more conventional to classrooms, are sparked in that way and take on new importance for students who are not natural academicians.

Of course, instruction can not always be planned to incorporate the action, variety, and concrete experiences described in these examples. Type concepts can also help you plan better instruction when you are limited largely to the classroom and media center. The table on pages 70-71, developed by Margaret Morgan, shows the classroom learning styles for each of the 16 types. Note that in the table sensing types are described as linear learners, and intuitives as global learners. Linear refers to the step-by-step, sequential approach to learning tasks. The global approach involves intuitive leaps, seeking to see the whole of the task first. Also note the preferences of different types for various media of instruction. These preferences are confirmed by research reported by McCaulley and Natter.[*]

Even the most routine aspects of classroom instruction (drill is an example) can be infused with some concrete action to make them more appealing. When drill on reading and writing and other skills is needed, the class can be shifted into two-person teams. Team members can choose each other (for example, by writing first, second and third choices on a piece of paper) or ask to be assigned to someone. Teams should keep the same membership for several weeks, with the teacher cancelling a team or changing team composition as needed. During team time, members can decide whether to, and when to work together or separately; and how much time to spend in either arrangement. Some teachers give the students the option of handing in joint work or separate products. The point is that two kinds

[*]M. H. McCaulley and F. L. Natter, "Psychological (Myers-Briggs) Type Differences in Education," in F. L. Natter and S. A. Rollins, Editors, **The Governor's Task Force on Disruptive Youth, Phase II-Report.** Tallahassee: Office of the Governor of Florida, 1974, p. 146f.

of accountability need to be maintained: the individual student's responsibility to the teacher (and him/herself), and team members' accountability to each other. If the team members have been taught type concepts and know each other's type, they can use that data to communicate more easily in the process of trying to be accountable.

Adjusting Instruction for T F and J P Differences

When the basic instruction plan has been made, in terms of ES, EN, IS and IN preferences, you then can consider the T F and J P dimensions. You can use this list of "needs" that are usually associated with T F and J P differences.

J 1. A need for **structure** and **predictability** is much more common among **J**'s than **P**'s. IS__J students need it most. If **J** students do not have their own structure for schoolwork worked out, the teacher must provide it. They value an **orderly sequence** of studies. **J**'s can be comfortable with some variety and spontaneity if they know that an underlying structure is intact or that the structure actually calls for those things.

J 2. A need for **mileposts,** for **completions** and a sense of **closure** is also a **J** characteristic. Progress charts and other tangible records are useful. Ceremonies, even little ones, to mark successful completions are valued, as are traditions generally. Persistence is a related **J** trait, and ceremonies that honor successful persistence will be especially appreciated. (In contrast, persistence does not come easily to **P**'s, but they need to develop it. The ceremonies are likely to benefit them, too.)

J 3. **J**'s need a **system of accountability** that is clear and made known in advance. They want to know what they are accountable for, when, how, and by what standards they will be judged. **J**'s will learn out of a sense of duty, for a while at least; but that is not a good substitute for clear expectations made known in advance.

P 4. A need for **variety, novelty and change** is one of the characteristics most common to **P** types. As McCaulley and Natter note, the typically structured classroom "can make the perceptive types feel imprisoned, with the result that they spend energy needed for study trying to get freedom. More flexible classrooms are naturally more suited to these students."

P 5. A need for **autonomy** and real **choice** is strong in **P**'s. The need is especially strong in __N__**P**'s. They work much better at tasks they have chosen. They will accept structure and a system of accountability if they have choices within the structure, and especially if they have had a hand in deciding and protecting the structure. For example, a system of individual contracts, in which a student can negotiate some activities, is a structure **P**'s would enjoy planning and supporting.

P   6.   **P**'s need opportunities to be **spontaneous** and free-wheeling, to follow their **curiosity.** The teacher alert to this need will find tasks for **P**'s that let them explore and find new facts or possibilities for the class to use.

T   7.   Thinking type students have a need for **order,** if order is taken to mean that logic rules the situation. They resent order that is not logical. The teacher should prompt **T**'s to take leadership in analyzing confused situations, to use their logic to make the situations orderly, and to spell out logical consequences.

T   8.   **T**'s need to **achieve,** to have a **sense of mastery,** and they need intellectual achievement more than **F**'s. This need is a natural ally to the school's objectives. Many **T** children don't know what they can master, what skills they can develop to the mastery level, and they need very specific help in this. Without help, some of them will find mastery in anti-school behavior, because the need for mastery is much stronger than the need to please people—including teachers. For the majority of the **T**'s, mastery is most likely to be found in mechanical and technical areas, many of which are unfortunately unavailable for students to explore until they reach high school.

T   9.   **T**'s have a need to **endure,** to **persist,** to **prevail** in things they are committed to. They want to have the last word in arguments. They may choose the wrong things to persist in, and they often need help in identifying the values that really are most worthy of their stick-to-it-iveness. Teachers can avoid useless confrontation with **T** students by recognizing early signs of persistent resistance and redirecting the students' thinking power into careful **analysis** of the situation, looking for cause and effect relationships. (Teacher: "We seem to disagree. Tell me how you see the problem . . . Have you thought about it from this angle . . .?")

F 10.   Feeling type students' need for **approval and personal support** is stronger than their need to achieve, to prevail, or to be "right." In some **F** students it is much stronger. Teachers who emphasize independent, individualized activities for students should be especially careful that they have not cut off **F** students from one of their main sources of motivation: the sense that their work is valued and appreciated. They want warm, not cool or impersonal acknowledgment of their work.

F 11.   F's need to be **needed,** to know that they are **helpful** to peers and adults. They are turned off by assignments that seem to have no particular value to anyone except to themselves in some impersonal, remote sense (as with the memorization of many facts and skills that are found in textbooks). Receiving the teacher's personal support and approval does not adequately substitute for the student's need to be helpful. So feeling types are most likely to profit from work in a harmonious group—when the task involves group members in helping each other, with a division of labor and shared responsibility. Examples would be group projects, tutoring, team learning and drilling with a partner. Projects that have a goal of being helpful to people **outside** the classroom are especially motivating to **F** students. They may even warm up to more remote materials if the human side is presented first.

F 12.   The need for **friendship** is especially strong in feeling types. They value harmony and will give in on disagreements because they want to preserve satisfying personal relationships. If the teacher will give them the opportunity to call attention to disharmony in the classroom, **F** students can be very helpful in leading the class toward an improved classroom climate. Most important of all to many **F** students is the opportunity to work with a friend. Friends who work together generally will stay on task if they know they will be separated when they abuse the opportunity. Peer affiliation is probably the most powerful force inside middle schools and high schools. The wise teacher harnesses it and doesn't try to fight it.

Plan a Unit of Instruction Using Type Concepts

If you have a colleague or two with whom you can share your plan, this planning sequence may be helpful to you.

1.   Select one classroom group of students with which to try using type concepts. As needed, coordinate your choice of students and your instruction plans with other people.
2.   If your students are 12 years or older, decide whether to administer the Myers-Briggs Type Indicator to them. If you decide to do so, precede the administering of it with an introduction to the idea, such as the "People Types and Tiger Stripes" activity. The introduction should serve to spark students' interest in the instrument so they will respond to it seriously. Some students will have difficulty with the instrument because of its reading level. Reading the items orally to them is an op-

36

tion. If you do read the items to them, each student should have a copy of the Indicator to look at as you read. Do not interpret questions for them. Take care to make the choices of each question sound equally desirable. Have them skip items they don't understand. After they take the MBTI, be sure they have their profile interpreted and their questions answered. Nearly all the students will be keenly interested in their profiles.

3. Decide whether to have the students respond to the four lists entitled, "I Am Likely to Do My Best Work . . ." Steps two and three are intended to give you some evidence of the types of your students. Having information on that is not essential to this planning sequence, but it is helpful. If you have students who cannot read the Indicator or the other materials, it is possible to recognize characteristics of type in their behavior. In the next chapter is a set of observation checklists by which you can estimate students' types by observing the patterns in their behavior. The process is time-consuming but may fit your needs. Once again, knowing each student's type is not essential to planning instruction with type concepts.

4. Prepare a plan of instruction—either a new plan you have not implemented before, or a revision of a plan you have used before. This plan will incorporate type concepts, following the three-step process described earlier in this chapter. Prepare it in sufficient detail so that your colleagues can read it and probably follow its intent without having to ask you for clarification on major points. If you prefer, you can prepare a joint plan with one or more partners. In either case, your plan should have a clear rationale based on type concepts.

5. Decide what data you can gather, as progress reports or a final report at the end of the unit, to show tangibly how well your plan worked. If you do succeed in making a better match between students and the learning setting, what would you expect to improve? Student time-on-task can be estimated by simple observation. Student interest can be sampled by a few questionnaire items. Student achievement can be documented by student products and by teacher-made tests. Organize these ideas into an evaluation plan.

6. Before you implement your plan, have your colleague(s) review it, critique its applications of type concepts, and make suggestions.

CHAPTER THREE

DEVELOPMENTAL NEEDS AND TYPE CONCEPTS

Promoting achievement of skills and knowledge is the first goal of American schools. Helping students develop as integrated persons is another goal. The realities of schooling are such that achievement gets virtually all the attention and development gets almost none. One reason for the imbalance is that teachers have many practical models to follow for promoting achievement, but very few models for helping students with development needs. Type concepts, as yet unknown to most educators, are a practical resource that teachers can use to help individual students in their development of perspective, judgment, perception and flexibility.

Each type has strengths and weaknesses

Strengths and weaknesses in people, as shown by type theory, come in patterns. By analyzing students in terms of type concepts, you can get some insights into their strengths and weaknesses and get clues to use in planning ways to help them develop. Consider Lisa, for example, who was described in the Introduction to the book. Reread the two paragraphs about Lisa. Now that you know about type concepts, what type would you say Lisa is? Extraversion is obvious (talkative, gregarious). The friendliness and the desire to be helpful and popular strongly suggest a feeling process at work. The other preferences are harder to detect in this brief description. Here is a speculation. The easy rapport with others suggests a sensing-feeling combination. A preference for S and F is further indicated by her choosing to avoid complexities and her difficulty in getting an objective perspective on herself. Because she wants very much to be helpful and be accepted, but then misses the mark and annoys her friends, she may be a judging type—so intent on ends that she neglects the means. Since her own motives seem to her to be so pure, the hurt and resentment she experiences from criticism further supports the feeling-judging choice. Lisa, then, is probably an Extraverted-Feeling type, ESFJ.

If Lisa is indeed an ESFJ, how does that identification help us think about her personal development needs? There are two fairly easy techniques for starting the process. First consider the type that is opposite hers, INTP. In general INTP's strengths are ESFJ's weaknesses, and vice versa.

What INTP does well naturally, ESFJ probably does least well. In **Introduction to Type** read the description of INTP (page 10) and see if you think Lisa's weaknesses seem to be INTP strengths. When you examine the profile of the opposite type you can better see the pattern and range of the strengths and weaknesses of the type you are trying to help.

The second technique for analyzing strengths and weaknesses is to look at the person's "zig-zag" process. Zig-zag refers to the sequence in which we use the four processes—S, N, T and F—in solving a problem.

The sequence begins with sensing. When faced with a problem, we properly start by gathering relevant, concrete data through the senses. The raw data by themselves do not settle the problem. The meaning of the data, their relationships to prior experience, are given by intuition—so the arrow goes from S to N. Intuition also asks: What are the possibilities in these data for solving the problem? The arrow moves from N to T when we engage thinking to analyze and decide the logical consequences of acting upon each of the possibilities. And finally the possibilities are also weighed by feeling-judgment to assess how deeply we care about the effects of each option; we test the human consequences, the harmony with basic personal values, or the values of others. A mature settling of the problem will have involved the four processes in a balanced way. But, of course, each type plays favorites with the four processes, and balance is difficult to achieve.

In Lisa's situation, the imbalance favors feeling, her dominant process, and sensing, her auxiliary process (Remember? An E___J's favorite process is one of the two kinds of judgment—F in Lisa's case—and the extravert uses the favorite process in the outside world). So an ESFJ gives most attention to feeling and second most attention to sensing. Lisa's zig-zag would look like this:

$$S \longrightarrow N$$
$$T \longleftarrow \mathbf{F}$$

The unbalancing power of her **F** is pulling her mental processes too quickly through **N**, zipping past **T** and coming to rest in a comfortable feeling judgment; but the judgment, unfortunately, is based on too few raw data (S), consideration of too few possibilities (N) inadequately analyzed (T). So Lisa seems flighty and her work is described as trite and shallow. A mature

ESFJ, on the other hand, has learned to use all four processes appropriately.

Lisa needs especially to give more time to sensing and then to develop her intuition and thinking. What can be done to help her? The first principle in a helping strategy is: use a strength to strengthen a weakness. The message or action of a teacher that will have the most influence with Lisa is one that will appeal to her feeling process, her strongest process. Her E __ F __ combination means she has a very strong need to be accepted, to maintain harmonious relations with her friends. The need impels her to be very good at friendly talk and maintaining easy rapport. How can she use this strength to strengthen her weaknesses? Here are a few ideas:

1. Next time she is rebuffed by a friend, the teacher can ask her, "What was your friend feeling when she criticized you? What happened just before? What were you feeling just before?" The objective is for her to tune more precisely into clues about her friends' feelings, to sharpen her perception and to stay longer in the perceptive mode. The place to show her the value of improved perception is in an area of great importance to her—her status with her friends.

2. She is likely to do much better schoolwork when teamed with a classmate friend whose perception is better developed than her own, perhaps an ES__P. The guidelines for two-person teams in the previous chapter should be helpful. Schoolwork that permits extraverting seems more likely to help Lisa develop her sensing more fully. If the assignments she is given require thinking and reflection (introversion), the teamwork dialogue should stimulate her to do both thinking and reflecting better than she would when working silently by herself.

3. Some exercises for listening skills—such as perception checking and paraphrasing—would appeal to her ESF__ nature and would strengthen her S.

4. She needs and will respond to honest praise much better than to criticism. She probably would receive and give attention to positive suggestions when they follow praise but not when they are couched in criticism.

5. Lisa probably would respond to values clarification activities that ask her to recognize values implicit in her behavior, force her to make value choices and have her affirm her values to her schoolmates. The teacher should select valuing activities that are not too vague and open-ended. Lisa is a J, remember.

6. The teacher could assign tasks to Lisa that progressively require and reward greater amounts of commitment and risk-taking. The natural step beyond value clarification is commitment and action on the priority values that have become clear.

Type Development Analysis

The process used for analyzing Lisa's situation can be applied to anyone. Here are brief descriptions° of four more situations of students with which you can test your ability to recognize type and to prescribe actions to help the students' development. Read each of the descriptions (enclosed in a box), decide what type formula fits the student, and circle the appropriate letters. Then on a separate sheet, write a brief analysis of the kind that was done for Lisa, and identify several activities or teaching techniques that you recommend for helping the student. You can compare your analysis and recommendations with those of the authors, which follow each box.

E   I

      Jan is conscientious and hard working, but often seems silent and remote.

S   N   She usually works very hard, but sometimes accomplishes surprisingly little. At times her work is totally off-target. She doesn't even try to make

T   F   others understand what she's doing, or why, and most people have given up trying to understand her and leave her alone.

J   P

Jan

Jan sounds like an **Introverted Sensing** type, ISTJ, with insufficient judgment. Her remoteness suggests introversion and thinking. Conscientiousness suggests sensing and judging. That her judgment is poorly developed can be detected in her work. She plods along without analyzing her work (a lack of thinking judgment); and she does not tune in to other people's values, and may be unclear about her own priorities (a lack of feeling judgment).

1. Only specific, detailed suggestions have a chance of impressing her. Advice not carefully worked out will seem like meddlesome interference to this independent type.
2. Her perseverance can lend stability to the group. This group need may be one she can recognize as making sense, and may motivate her to desire becoming part of the group.
3. Whenever possible, put her in charge of important routines, and arrange for her to work out the policies with others. Within the division of labor, help her obtain jobs that are clearly defined.
4. Peers should be encouraged to explain their motives as logically as possible to her, and expect that she do the same.
5. Role-playing simulations of how a communication should transpire

---

°Adapted from Nuernberger and Lawrence, **Personality Influences in Teaching and Learning**, pp. 43-48. By permission.

41

might be helpful. She can play the part of the person trying to understand Jan—perhaps she can even interview the person who is playing "Jan."

6. Jan will be encouraged by small victories. Any small progress she makes in the developmental tasks described above should be given prompt recognition.

```
E   I

S   N   Dean loves to entertain, and can and does keep the group amused and
        distracted. Consequently, his own basic skills are poorly developed,
T   F   because he's usually "on stage" instead of at work.

J   P
```

Dean

This one is easy! Fun-loving, out-going, adaptable describe a **sensing, feeling, perceptive extravert.** Dean is probably an **Extraverted sensing** type, ESFP, the type which has more trouble with academics than any other.

Of all the types, ESFP's are most attuned to the present moment. Dean probably does his off-task socializing because academic work seems too remote and abstract to him, and it fails to hold his attention.

1. If he is still having trouble with reading, check him out on phonics. If his background here is insufficient it may give this type particular trouble.

2. He learns by doing. The more sensory input he has, the greater the chance he will learn. Whenever possible, lessons should be multisensory. He may especially like a variety of media. Demonstrations and pictures mean far more to him than words or writing.

3. A lot of talk is apt to confuse him. Keep instructions to him simple and to the point. Don't expect him to read between the lines or come to conclusions without help.

4. Whenever possible, give him the responsibility of acting as arbiter for conflicting factions, and team him with people who will help him draw conclusions.

5. Glasser's *Reality Therapy* may help him clarify his goals and plan alternative behaviors.

6. Of this type it is especially true: "I hear, and I forget. I see, and I remember. I do, and I learn."

7. Self-management and time management techniques will also enhance his judgment.

E	I	John is hasty in voicing conclusions and he hurries on to new tasks before
S	N	old ones are completed. Action for the sake of action seems to be his approach to everything. Although he often shows a lack of concern for
T	F	the rights of others, he seems sincerely sorry when reproached about his transgressions. However, he seems to make the same blunders over and
J	P	over, and his teacher wonders if there is any hope for him.

John

Since he is described as active, quick to voice conclusions, he is probably an **extravert.** His rush to reach conclusions shows that he is probably a **judging** type, but **J**'s are more likely to finish what they begin. If his haste is due to an intolerance of complexity, he may be a sensing type, but if his hurry to new activities is due to having more ideas and inspirations than he can control, he is probably an intuitive. Neither thinking nor his feeling judgments seem adequately developed, a real handicap for a judging type.

Because he has a positive attitude to work in general, a lot of energy and a desire to accomplish things, John has a lot of good things going for himself. His "life-field" would look like this:

FORCE FIELD ANALYSIS

John's Life Field

Forces for		Forces against
1. Energy		1. Jumps to conclusions
2. Interest in activity		2. Leaves work incomplete
3. Quickness	John's effectiveness	3. Behaves "blindly"
4. Desire for accomplishments		4. Seems purposeless
5. Sympathy for others		5. Behaves inconsiderately

With these data, it is hard to see John's type. His forces against (1, 3 and 5) suggest a **lack of perception,** and (2 and 4) a **lack of judgment.** It is quite likely that his teachers' inability to understand him is due to their being very different types. It is apparent that his education has not been effective for him. If his compulsive activity is an effort to please someone who does not understand him very well, he is probably a feeling type and suffers a lot from not being understood.

John

John's teacher probably should begin with a plan which takes into consideration the possibility that he is an extravert in a judging life-style, and attempt to gather more data about his preferred processes. In the meantime, he will benefit from:

1. Learning activities which allow action and free movement.
2. Activities which have as their aim specific standards, criteria, consequences and products, which are made clear to him in the beginning.
3. Learning to state his own behavioral objectives when undertaking new learnings.
4. Being teamed with very perceptive types, who can also benefit from the collaboration.
5. Learning listening techniques, such as paraphrasing and summarizing what has been said.
6. Carefully outlining and planning each project in detailed sequence.

E	I	
S	N	Bob has little self-confidence. He almost never volunteers a response in class, except privately to the teacher, after class is all over, because he isn't sure he's right. He often undertakes projects of such complexity that failure is almost certain, even though he is willing to work long and hard. It almost seems as though he were his own worst enemy and critic.
T	F	
J	P	

Bob

Shyness and a preference for complexity suggest **introversion** and **intuition,** and the long devotion to undertaken projects is characteristic of the **feeling** types. Because his vision is broad, he is probably a **perceptive** type. Bob, then, is an **Introverted Feeling** type, INFP.

1. Busywork is not for him. He must feel there is an important purpose in which he believes behind the work he does. He should do well with a contract plan in which he can choose some materials and activities for himself.
2. Teach him goal clarification techniques, and show him how to break his large over-all goals into small, component, sequential goals which can be evaluated independently of each other.
3. Teach him evaluation techniques so that he can objectively assess his own work.
4. His confidence will be bolstered if he is shown the evidence of real benefits to others which are the results of his own efforts, even though the results fall short of his own expectations.

5. Teach him to check his plans with an opposite type who will tactfully question him about details and sequences.
6. He will benefit from uninterrupted periods of intense work on a single project, and from frequent and sincere statements of appreciation and support.

Lisa, Jan, Dean, John, and Bob had at least one thing in common: their achievement of school objectives was being blocked by difficulties in their development—what teachers in earlier times called character development. If you now have some students who need help as these did, you can follow the process shown in the analysis of Lisa's situation. Try the process with at least two students.

1. Write a paragraph or two describing their basic traits;
2. Identify their types (guess if you need to);
3. Analyze their strengths and weaknesses based on type descriptions;
4. Analyze their zig-zags; and
5. Make a list of things that could be done to help them in their development. We suggest *Introduction to Type* as a resource for this task, particularly pages 4, 5, 17 and 18.

Many teachers have also found that ideas for activities come to them when they scan a list of judgment and perception terms such as this one:

ACTIVITIES THAT TEACH CHILDREN TO USE THEIR MENTAL PROCESSES:

Judgment	Perception
goal clarification	communicating
values clarification	observing
managing time	listening
choosing	smelling
deciding	touching
organizing	summarizing
criticizing	imagining
analyzing	collecting (data)
empathizing	investigating

Both perception and judgment

classifying	applying (concepts)
finding relationships	designing (projects)
interpreting	evaluating
hypothesizing	taking risks

45

Examples of lessons that promote perception and judgment can be found in many sources. Two important sources are:

1. *Teaching for Thinking*, Raths and others, and
2. *Values and Teaching*, Raths, Harmin, and Simon (both published by Charles Merrill Co.).

On the next eight pages are checklists you can use to infer students' types from their overt behavior. If the students you choose to analyze are not able to read the MBTI, the checklists are a useful substitute. Teachers who know type concepts and who know their students well can make reasonable guesses about their types.

Observing For Evidences of Type*

Directions: Put student's name at top and put a check mark in each box opposite a phrase that describes him or her. Comparing tallies of E and I, S and N, T and F, J and P can give you an estimation of the person's type.

---

*Adapted from Nuernberger and Lawrence, **Personality Influences in Teaching and Learning**, Pp. 52-59. By permission.

STUDENT NAME

If your student is an EXTRAVERT, it is likely that he or she:

chooses to work with others, with large groups

plunges into new experiences, working by trial and error

is relaxed and confident

readily talks over events and ideas with others

is interested in other people and their doings

readily offers opinions

shares personal experiences

wants to experience things so as to understand them

is enthusiastic about activities involving action

asks questions to check on the expectations of the group or teacher

has a relatively short attention span

dislikes complicated procedures and gets impatient with slow jobs

is interested in the results of the job, in getting it done, and in how other people do it

eagerly attends to interruptions

acts quickly, sometimes without thinking

likes to have people around

communicates well and greets people easily

47

STUDENT NAME

If your student is an INTROVERT, it is likely that he or she:

chooses to work alone or with one person

holds back from new experiences

chooses written assignments over oral presentations

performs better in written work than in oral presentations

pauses before answering, and shows discomfort with spontaneous questioning

asks questions to allow understanding something before attempting to do it

is hard to understand, quiet and shy; seems "deep"

is intense, bottling up emotions

prefers setting his/her own standards when possible

goes from considering to doing and back to considering

has a small number of carefully selected friends

likes quiet space to work

works intently on the task at hand

works on one thing for a long time

prefers jobs that can be done "inside the head"

dislikes interruptions

likes to think a lot before acting, sometimes doesn't act at all

STUDENT NAME

If your student prefers SENSING, it is likely that he or she:

is realistic and practical

is intensely aware of the environment

is more observant than imaginative

is pleasure loving and contented

is possessive of things, a consumer

is imitative; prefers memorizing rather than finding out reasons

changes moods as physical surroundings change

learns best from an orderly progression of sequential details

brings up pertinent facts

keeps accurate track of details, makes lists

is patient

is good at checking, inspecting, "reading the fine print," and precise work

dislikes new problems unless there are standard ways to solve them

likes an established routine

enjoys using skills already learned more than learning new ones

works steadily all the way through to a conclusion, not having bursts of energy and slack periods

is impatient or frustrated with complicated situations

doesn't usually get inspirations and doesn't trust inspirations

STUDENT NAME

If your student prefers INTUITION it is likely that he or she:

craves inspiration

is more imaginative than observant

pays more attention to the whole concept than to details

is aware of only the personally relevant aspects of the external environment

becomes restless, impatient with routines

is an initiator, promoter, inventor of ideas

sees possibilities that others miss

is quick with finding solutions

doesn't always "hear you out;" is impatient with all sustained sensing occupations

is indifferent to what others own or consume

looks far ahead, furnishes new ideas

likes spotting problems and solving them

dislikes doing the same thing over

enjoys learning a new skill more than using it

works in bursts of energy, and has slack periods in between

jumps to conclusions; makes factual errors

follows inspirations good or bad

dislikes taking time for precision

STUDENT NAME

If your student prefers THINKING, it is likely that he or she:

is logical and analytical

is impersonal, impartial

is more interested in ideas or things than in human relationships

is more truthful than tactful

is stronger in executive ability than in the social arts

is brief and businesslike

takes very seriously facts, theories, and the discovery of truth

takes seriously the solution of practical problems

treats emotional relationships and ideals quite casually

contributes intellectual criticism

exposes wrongs in the habits, customs, and beliefs of others

is offended by illogic in others

holds firmly to a policy or conviction

hurts other people's feelings without knowing it

doesn't need harmony

decides things impersonally, sometimes ignoring people's wishes

is upset by injustice

seems not to know how his or her own actions affect other people's feelings

STUDENT NAME

If your student prefers FEELING, it is likely that he or she:

is personal, likes personal relationships

is more interested in people than things or ideas

is more tactful than truthful, if forced to choose

is likely to agree with others in the group

thinks as others think, believing them probably right

finds it difficult to be brief and businesslike

takes emotional relationships and ideals very seriously

is offended by a lack of personal consideration in others

is motivated by others

is compliant

permits feelings to override logic

forecasts how others will feel

arouses enthusiasm

is upset by conflicts; values harmony

dislikes telling people unpleasant things

relates well to most people

is sympathetic

STUDENT NAME

If your student is a JUDGING type, it is likely that he or she:

has his or her mind made up

is more decisive than curious

lives according to plans

lives according to standards and customs not easily or lightly set aside

tries to make situations conform to his or her own standards, "the way they ought to be."

makes definite choices from among the possibilities

is uneasy with unplanned happenings

bases friendship upon beliefs, standards and tastes which are assumed to be shared

has enduring friendships

sees more perceptive people as aimless drifters, unmoral if not immoral

aims to be right

is self-regimented, purposeful and exacting

is orderly, organized and systematic

perseveres

has settled opinions

is tolerant of routine

STUDENT NAME

If your student is a PERCEPTIVE type, it is likely that he or she:

is more curious than decisive

lives according to the situation of the moment

may not plan things, acts spontaneously

is masterful in handling the unplanned, unexpected, or incidental

is empirical and dependent on experience

amasses vast quantities of experiences, more than can be digested or used

is uncritical

bases friendships on propinquity and shared experience

easily and often drops friendships, forgets them, resumes them

aims to miss nothing

is flexible, adaptable and tolerant

is understanding and open-minded

leaves things open

has trouble making decisions

starts too many projects and has difficulty in finishing them

postpones unpleasant jobs

welcomes new light on a thing, situation or person

54

Type Development: An Educational Objective[*]

Education requires students to take in something new, and to decide how to use what they have learned. In terms of type theory, students must learn to perceive accurately, they must learn how to observe, how to pay attention to the facts and details of their environment (i.e., to use their sensing). They must also learn how to fit experience together into new patterns, to see what things mean, to open up new possibilities, to use imagination (i.e., to use their intuition). In making decisions, students need to learn when it is appropriate to be objective, analytical, and to weigh the consequences of their actions (i.e., to make thinking judgments). At other times, they need to know how to use their own values, to weigh the relative importance of long range alternatives to themselves and/or other people (i.e., to make feeling judgments).

In type development, we assume all students need to learn good command of sensing, intuition, thinking and feeling. For each type, two of these processes come more easily and more naturally, and two are uphill work. Teachers who understand type can help students discover their own natural bent. Then, they can go on to help them develop expertness in use of the four mental processes—first, by stretching their abilities in the processes that come most easily to them and have the most intrinsic interest, and later, by becoming at least passably good in the others.

Furthermore, schools can help students learn when to use the four attitudes: When it is useful to extravert and pay attention to what is going on in the environment, and when it is useful to introvert and pay attention to the inner world of thoughts and contemplation. Extraverted children can be helped to extravert effectively, but to enjoy their own company and thoughts. Introverted children can be given more time to work alone and to go into depth in studies, but can also be encouraged to learn the skills of extraverting—in the interest of having more experiences to think about. Judging children can learn how to develop their sense of order into effective study habits, but can also learn when it is better to keep an open mind and to stay curious and receptive (remain in the perceptive attitude). Perceptive children can be shown how to develop their open curiosity about the world, but can also learn when it is better to stop perceiving and make a decision. . . .

Different types of educators are naturally most concerned with the aspects of type development closest to their own type. Traditionalists (*sensing-thinking-judging*) are demanding discipline and the fundamental 3 R's. Humanists (*intuitive-feeling-perceptive*) are encouraging free (unstruc-

---

[*]McCaulley and Natter, "Psychological (Myers-Briggs) Type Differences in Education," Pp. 204-209. By permission.

tured) school models with "open" classrooms and curriculum. Unfortunately, both camps may fail to see that no single approach will be effective with all types of students. Rather than downplaying the qualities valued by the other, both approaches could develop educational experiences to meet the needs of all types of students.

Jung's terminology may seem strange at first, but the processes he was describing are familiar to all good teachers. Behavior management looks at what the child is actually doing—noticing the facts (*sensing*) of his outer behavior (*extraversion*), and then finding a way to reward him (by giving something his *feeling* values) to organize his life (use *judging* attitude) in a more effective way. When we use reality therapy, we ask the child "What are you doing (use your *sensing* to see what the situation is), what really matters to you (what is your best *feeling* judgment on this matter), and where is this behavior taking you (what does your *thinking* tell you of the consequences)?" When we ask students in career planning "What are the other possibilities you might consider?", we are saying "What does your *intuition* suggest?" When we ask "What really matters to you in the way you want to live and conduct your life?", we are asking, "What are your *feeling* judgments in this matter?" When we teach children to be open about what they are really feeling, we are asking them to *extravert*. When we ask them what is the idea that prompts a given statement, we are asking them to *introvert*. . . .

The point is that teachers and counselors are already trying to teach type development to students, though they do not necessarily use the terms or concepts of type theory. What type theory adds is an understanding of the road each person takes to excellence—which process will be interesting and easy for him, and which will be difficult. It is possible to use the learning activities of a school to provide challenges and problems that help all types develop, by busying their minds on tasks that engage all their abilities and not just on tasks they can do with half their attention, or while "spinning their wheels." As schools improve their capacity to help each type develop in its best way, we shall find less visible disruption, less silent disruption, and less underachievement. More important, we shall be training a group of citizens who can effectively direct their lives, and who have learned to value the important contributions of all types of people to the complex decisions of a democratic society.

CHAPTER FOUR

TYPE AND TEACHING STYLES

Teachers and researchers who understand type concepts see ample evidence that teachers' types do indeed affect the way they teach and what they prefer to teach.

1. Different types of teachers are attracted to different levels of schooling and to different subject matters. More S's than N's teach in elementary and middle school grades; they are about even in high school. The preferences for subject matters are predictable—e.g., T's for math, N's for theoretical courses, S's for practical courses, and F's for art and guidance.

2. Type differences influence the way a subject is taught—e.g., in social studies, S's tend to emphasize facts and biography and concrete skills, while N's emphasize concepts and relationships.

3. Teachers are more likely to understand and get along better with students of types similar to their own. Some students who are not very secure in themselves especially need teachers of similar type, with whom they can relate easily, and in whom they can find type-alike behaviors and attitudes to emulate. More secure students need the challenge of being with some teachers who are more unlike them in type so they can test and strengthen their weaker, less used processes.

4. In teaching style, introverted teachers tend toward securing the predictability they need by keeping control centered in themselves rather than decentralized, in individual student's hands. Introverts are more likely to structure activities through the materials they select for students, and less likely to give students choices of what to study or how to do it.

5. Sensing types tend toward keeping things centralized and limiting the range of student choices. They are less likely to move freely around the room than are the intuitives.

6. Feeling types generally differ from thinkers in several ways: having students focus attention on their own individual work and not on the teacher; having students work individually while the teacher moves from student to student attending to each closely, usually seeking some dialogue with each student; all the while being able to attend to more

than one student at a time. And **F**'s praise and criticize, support and correct students, by word and body language, more than **T**'s.

7. The classroom of the **I**, the **S** and the **J** is more likely to be quiet and orderly; and when students in those classrooms do get off task, they are apt to daydream, doddle and do other passive-withdrawn things. In contrast, the **E**, the **N** and the **P** teacher's classroom probably has more movement, more student decisions about what to do, more noise; and when students get off task, they most likely do it actively and noisily. And the **E**, **N** and **P** teacher spends more time trying to get the students settled down to work.

8. I _ _ J teachers seem to need most structure in the classroom; E _ _ J's need somewhat less, I _ _ P's less and E _ _ P's least of all. In fact, E _ _ P's seem to do things that will bring some unpredictability into the classroom: encourage open-ended discussion, ask students to create projects, permit socializing in study groups, etc. Clearly, the amount of structure a teacher needs for personal equilibrium will suit the needs that some students have for external structure and it will not fit others.

   Moreover, teachers' types influence their perceptions of how much external structuring their students need. Consider, for example, an I _ _ J and an E _ _ P, who are equally familiar with a group of 30 students. If asked to sort the students into three groups, according to their need for low, moderate and high amounts of external structure, the E _ _ P teacher is likely to classify fewer in the high category than is the I _ _ J.

   What are the implications for instruction? Asking teachers to change their need for structure is unrealistic. There are two alternatives: students are placed so as to obtain a better match between teacher style and student need for classroom structure; or teachers learn techniques for varying structure, techniques that do not force them beyond their own equilibrium. One **J** math teacher, for example, was able to divert his strong need for order and control away from overbearing supervision of students to an inanimate object. He constructed a long chart showing students names and all the math sub-objectives, and he exercised his **J** by moving markers on the chart. A **P** teacher who realized he was too unstructured for many students found the answer in individual student contracts. Students who needed more structure got more tightly drawn contracts. He also arranged for election of class officers. Students debated and decided on a set of class rules and the officers exercised the **J** responsibility of enforcing them.

9. The combination of types on a teaching team makes a difference in the team's productivity, compatibility and flexibility. A good mix of types is a strong asset to a team. Look at the type table on the last page of *Introduction to Type*. Does your team have three or four of

the columns (ST, SF, NF, NT) represented? Three or four quadrants, too (IS, ES, IN, EN)?

Read back through the nine sets of facts about teaching styles and consider your own teaching style in relation to your type. Analyze your own zig-zag. Do these analyses give you a new angle for looking at your strengths and weaknesses? Does the zig-zag give you some ideas of how to use your strengths to strengthen a weakness?

Type and Teacher-Teacher Relationships

You are already aware of many ways that type affects the relationships between teachers. Type concepts can also be used to analyze the complexities of relationships and make them more manageable. Here is a description of a conflict between two teachers. Using type concepts, analyze the conflict and consider what might be done to improve the relationship.

Two members of a teaching team frequently seem to have misunderstandings. Mr. Green is often the "idea man" of the team, suggesting with enthusiasm that the team try this or that. Generally his ideas seem sound to the team, but in need of some refinement and attention to practical details. Mrs. White, another team member, is usually the first one to question Mr. Green's ideas, on grounds of practicality, and she states her position in such a blunt way that she sometimes causes hard feelings. At that point, Mr. Green "clams up," and his idea fades away without the team dealing with it further. Outside of team planning meetings, Green and White seem to get along quite well. Analyze the Green-White relationship by answering these questions:

1. What types are Green and White (make a guess)?
2. How can you explain the conflict in terms of type theory?
3. Assuming you are a member of their team and felt a need to help them, what would you say privately to Green? To White? Write your remarks just as you would say them; put them in quotation marks.
4. Do you identify with either Green or White more than with the other? Would you be comfortable in the role of peacemaker between these two? Do your responses to these questions relate to your own type?

The Green-White situation will yield many more insights if you can discuss it with a colleague or two. After you have discussed it, you can compare your analysis and action plan with the one below.

Possible Actions for the Green-White Conflict

Chances are that Mrs. White doesn't even know she caused hard feelings. She is probably an __STJ. Say to her, in private, calmly and plainly, "I think you came across too strongly with Mr. Green. I'd say his feelings

59

are a fact to be reckoned with next time. Your knack for spotting quickly what is missing in a proposed plan is a real asset to the team. But I'll bet Mr. Green feels you never heard what he did say. He probably wouldn't be turned off if you said instead, 'Your plan might work if we figured out how to deal with this and this and this.' "

Mr. Green, full of interesting possibilities (**N**) not thought out completely (**P**), was hurt by the critical analysis (**F**) and retreated quickly to withdrawn silence (probably **I**—an **E** most likely would have argued and defended the plan). Privately, you can say to him, "I expect Mrs. White has no idea that she caused hard feelings. She's blunt, but I think her bluntness comes from her logic, not from her feelings. She certainly isn't alert to other people's feelings the way that you are."

Mr. Green "clams up" because he values harmony more than the life of his idea. You might say to him, "I think her __STJ is abrasive to your __NFP, but I would hate for those differences to freeze out your good ideas. Simply knowing that she is acting true to type might ease the friction for you. I think we can really benefit from her natural talent for homing in on missing details, or gaps in a plan. Maybe, if you have more details filled in next time, the team has a better chance of agreeing on your plan and we can go ahead with your good ideas."

Isabel Myers' essay that follows seems especially useful for understanding situations such as the Green-White conflict.

Type in Human Relations°

The effects of type in this field do not lend themselves easily to statistical verification but can be explored by personal observation and experience. The conclusions reached from the writer's observation and experience are therefore offered as a frame of reference for the reader's own explorations.

Recognition of the type differences, when carried over into the field of person-to-person relationships, may afford a useful system for understanding others whose attitudes or actions seem unreasonable.

Type theory would hold that type differences yield differences in interests, values, and problem-solving techniques which may facilitate or handicap a working relationship between two or more people. Where two individuals interacting with one another are of similar type, there is a better chance of communication of ideas. Sensing types like facts; intuitives like possibilities; thinkers like logical principles; feeling types like a human angle. A good sound idea can be presented in any or all of these forms, but

---

°Isabel Briggs Myers. **Manual (1962). The Myers-Briggs Type Indicator.** Palo Alto: Consulting Psychologists Press, 1975. By permission.

difficulties may be expected to occur if, say, the thinker attempts to force logical reasons upon a feeling type or possibilities upon the sensing people.

It has seemed to the writer that most people get around this difficulty by picking friends mainly from their own type column, a fact generally apparent if one enters his friends upon a Type Table. In marriage there is a significant tendency to prefer likeness to difference, especially on SN. But parents and children have no option. They are stuck with each other's types, for better or worse.

The type differences, and the resulting family conflicts, can appear very early. A six-year-old girl with feeling said in dismay after a week's visit from a five-year-old thinker, "He doesn't care about **pleasing,** does he?" Basically, he never will. He has to have reasons. The small feeling type will do things for the sake of "pleasing" but is quite unmoved by logic. If one expects to influence either, he must give him a motivation that means something to his type.

As individuals grow up, each type can profit by learning how to get along with the other. The thinker is by nature impersonal and critical. He likes effects to follow logically from causes, and he forgets to reckon illogical human motives and reactions among the causes. In any disagreement, therefore, he tends to state his position bluntly, without concern for the feelings of the other people involved. The effect is to stir up antagonism which makes agreement needlessly hard.

Feeling types, on the other hand, set great value upon harmony and good feeling and are very aware of the likes and dislikes of the people around them. They assume that the thinker is equally aware, and resent his tactlessness toward others as well as toward themselves.

What the feeling types need to remember is that most of the time the thinker does not even know how people feel about things. He needs to be told, calmly and plainly, before trouble starts, so that he can count people's feelings among the causes to be reckoned with and act accordingly.

What the thinker needs to remember is that the feeling types prize harmony and really prefer to agree with him if given a chance. He should start every discussion by mentioning the points on which **he** agrees with **them.** If they can feel that he is basically in the same camp with them, they are ready to make concessions to preserve that harmony and stay in the same camp. The points of difference can then be discussed rather than fought over. And the thinker's logic and the feeling type's understanding of people can both be brought to bear upon the problem.

Clashes between the types arise out of the very fact that makes opposite types mutually useful to each other; the fact that each sees the side of the problem which the other naturally overlooks. For instance, the intuitive is by nature a thinker-upper; the sensing type a getter-doner. The sensing type puts his faith in the actual; the intuitive in the possible. When

61

an intuitive comes up with a blazing new idea, his natural course is to present it in rough and sketchy form, trusting his listener to concentrate on the main point and ignore the unworked-out details. The sensing type's natural reaction is to concentrate on what is missing, decide the idea won't work (which it won't in that form), and flatly turn it down. Result: one wasted idea and much hard feeling.

Either type could avoid the collision by a little respect for his opposite. The intuitive should be realistic enough to foresee the sensing type's reaction and prepare for it, work out the details of his project, and get together the necessary facts in unescapable form. The sensing type on his part should concede the intuitive's idea a fighting chance. He can say, "It might work if——" and then bring up all the objections that experience suggests and ask, "What would you do about this and this and this?" The intuitive then spends his energies happily against the obstacles, changing his ideas as necessary, and often ends with a solution valuable to them both.

When compromise between opposite types is necessary, the best compromise is that which preserves to each party the advantage he considers most important. The sensing type wants the solution to be workable, the thinker wants it systematic, the feeling type wants it humanly agreeable, and the intuitive wants a door left open for growth and improvement. People often go to the mat for a scheme as a whole, when what they really care about is one particular merit that could as well be incorporated into another plan.

Whenever people differ, a knowledge of type helps to cut out irrelevant friction. More than that, it points up the advantages of the differences. No one man has to be good at everything. He only has to be good at his own stuff and decently appreciative of the other fellow's. Together, thanks to their differences, they can do a better job than if they were just alike.

CHAPTER FIVE

TAKING TYPE INTO ACCOUNT IN EDUCATION

Isabel Briggs Myers

Schools are being told that they are accountable for educating every child. They are required to teach the basic **skills,** so that every child grows up able to read, write and balance a checkbook. And they are required to plant various sorts of **knowledge,** deeply enough so that it will germinate, take root and bear fruit.

Both demands are better met if the schools take into account the type differences among children. These are not quantitative differences that can be expressed simply as a higher or lower degree of mental ability. They are qualitative differences, differences as to the kind of perception and the kind of judgment that the child **prefers** to use. It is his preferences that make his type. Children of different types have a different "mix" of abilities, different needs, interests and motivations, and different degrees of success in school.

The preference that has the most conspicuous consequences in education is the choice between the two kinds of perception, the choice between sensing and intuition. Sensing focuses interest and attention upon the concrete reality that is apparent to the five senses. Sensing children are more interested in **doing** something, almost anything, with almost any tangible object, than in listening to what anyone is saying unless it has to do with action or adds something definite to their picture of the physical world. In contrast, intuition focuses interest and attention upon the end results of one's own unconscious processes, which include the translation of symbols —words into meaning, and meaning into words. Intuitive children thus tend to take a positive interest in language, spoken or written, and acquire a facility that is convenient in class and in verbal ability tests and also enables them to state clearly and usefully to themselves the relationships and possibilities suggested by their intuition.

It is therefore understandable that, as most schools are now run, sensing children have less use for school than intuitive children do (often no use at all), that on the average they make lower grades and score lower on intelligence tests (though not enough lower to account for their grades), and that they far more frequently drop out.

63

If we are to have a system of universal education that does justice to all the types, I think we must draw a sharp distinction between skills and knowledge. Knowledge spreads over a tremendous variety of subjects, each of which may be interesting and useful to certain types and a waste of time to others. But the basic skills are essential for all the types, and should be taught in such a way as to give every child what he needs.

The usual first grade has a substantial majority of sensing children and a smaller number of intuitives. The sensing children do not want to have to cope with anything unexplainable. The intuitives do not want to be bored by anything tedious and dull. Except for an occasional child who may have been let into the secret by an intuitive parent or have found it out for himself, none of the children, sensing or intuitive, know that letters stand for sounds.

In most first grades, nobody (for a long time) tells them this one crucial fact that makes sense of the process of learning to read. Reading thus consists of memorizing "sight words", recognizable only by their general shape. A new word is an insoluble mystery until teacher tells you what it is. Content is necessarily restricted to repetition of the few words thus far memorized. "Dick. See Dick. See Dick run." This method of teaching manages to frustrate both the sensing children and the intuitives. Reading, which ought to be a magical extension of one's own experience, is both unexplainable **and** dull.

To meet the needs of the sensing children who want things to be explicit and the intuitive children who want unlimited possibilities, first grades should introduce intensive phonics at the very beginning, so that every child in the class knows that there is a perfectly good way to tell what new words are. He is going to be able to read, very soon, up to the limits of his speaking vocabulary. And removal of the artificial limits on vocabulary means that he can read vastly more interesting things. He can, in fact, attempt anything he cares to tackle.

From the standpoint of the child's success in school and his development as a person, with ambition, initiative, and confidence in himself, the start of first grade marks a crucial fork in the road. That is the point at which he decides either that school makes sense or that it does not, that it is interesting or boring, that he can or cannot do these new things. If he cannot do the new things, his only defense against the humiliation of being "dumb" is to decide that such things are not worth doing.

The pitfall in the teaching of arithmetic skills is basically the same as the pitfall in teaching reading. The children who try to cope with the symbols without recognizing the realities these stand for are doomed to frustration. They never win through to the beautiful certainties in the realm of numbers. They just memorize incantations. "7 and 5 is 12." "11 minus 4 is 7." "5 times 7 is 35." When the teacher gives you the first two numbers of an incantation, you have to remember the third. If you forget that third number, there is nothing you can do about it. And if you are given a problem and can't see what kind of incantation to use, there is nothing you can do about **that.**

The solution is to establish the reality of numbers first. The symbols then can be understood as a way of talking about reality. There should be no operations with disembodied numerals, no incantations, no memorizing, no flash cards for "addition facts" and "subtraction facts", no verbal drill, until the children are thoroughly familiar with manual operations with quantities. To many sensing children, things you can touch and move are real but words are not.

The form in which a question is put can change the whole spirit of the proceedings. "How much is 7 and 5?" implies that the child ought to know by this time and the teacher wants to find out whether he does or not. This is wrong side to. The child is the one who should be doing the finding out. "Find out how much is 7 and 5!" is an invitation to action. Using number blocks, for instance, the child can take a block that is seven squares high and stand it against the number tower. Naturally it reaches to seven. Then he can take a block that is five squares high and stack it on top of the seven. Together they reach to twelve. Every time he does it they reach to twelve. In fact, he can see that they **have to** reach to twelve; the seven block is always three squares short of ten; the first three squares of the five block always get you to ten; the other two squares always stick up beyond ten and reach to twelve. A similar certainty has to exist in the case of 17 and 5, 27 and 5, and so on up.

Consistent use of this approach gives the child a picture of the number system as a whole, the place of any given number in that system, and its relation to other numbers. When he starts doing operations with numerals instead of blocks, he knows the quantities they stand for and what he is doing with those quantities. And when he is given a problem, he has a decent chance of seeing what he must do to solve it.

Reading, writing and arithmetic are well defined skills that every child needs to acquire. But **knowledge,** as distinguished from skills, is another matter. It has no limits. Schools must decide what tiny fraction they will try to teach. If we take it as axiomatic that a child should be taught things that are of lasting benefit to him, either by making him more effective or by otherwise enhancing his life, one brutal conclusion follows. There is no use in teaching a child things he intends to forget.

Nothing will stick in a child's mind long enough to do him any good unless it interests him, and here type plays a major role. The combination of a child's preferred kind of perception and his preferred kind of judgment tends to concentrate his interest in fields where these find scope, as shown in the comparison on page 3 of the *Introduction to Type.* His remaining preferences influence the kind of work he will like to do in those fields. Hence knowledge that is relevant, even illuminating, for a person with a given set of preferences can be acutely boring to a person with the opposite set. Aside from routine warnings against common dangers, like carbon monoxide and the signing of documents unread, there is probably no body of knowledge that can profitably be "taught" to every child regardless.

Time and effort spent in trying to teach a child something against his will are worse than wasted. Real harm is done. If a child is not interested in what he is supposed to be learning, he is bored. And the habit of being bored is disastrous for children, because it destroys their native curiosity. Babies and pre-schoolers have a great urge to make sense of the world. They devote their energies happily to finding out one thing after another, whatever fixes their curiosity at the moment. They learn at a tremendous rate, and they remember what they learn, because it becomes part of their world as they know it. Learning is high adventure, not a chore.

School should be a continuation of the adventure. Children in all the grades should be given maximum opportunity to learn the things that have meaning and interest for them in terms of their own kind of perception and their own kind of judgment. To the extent that they are given this opportunity, they gain not only in interest but in application and intelligence as well. People of any age, from six to sixty, apply themselves with greater vigor to the task in hand when they are interested. People of any age are more intelligent when they are interested than when they are bored.

A child permitted to study what interests him learns more and remembers it. The most valuable outcome, however, is the effect upon the **development** of his perception and judgment. A purposeful finding out about almost anything develops his perception. And a self-imposed doing of whatever is necessary to that end develops his judgment far more than would mere obedience to a teacher's authority. The lifelong importance of adequate development of perception and judgment is shown in past and current studies with the Type Indicator. Good perception and judgment are associated with achievement, which is reasonable because they make a person more effective in whatever he sets out to do. They are also associated with mental and physical health, which again is reasonable because they enable a person to cope more competently with his problems and thus lessen or eliminate strain.

Ways of making room for individual interests and study can be worked out in any school where authority will accept the idea. In fact, they can be worked out independently by any teacher. A seminar approach can be taken, in which the class is given a bird's-eye view of the different aspects of the subject and then allowed to sign up to work on whichever aspect each finds most interesting. Or a list of individual projects can be designed to appeal to widely different types. Flexibility can be achieved by framing some exam questions for sensing types, others for intuitives, everyone being permitted to leave out the two he likes least. Or it may be announced in advance that everyone may formulate and answer one question of his own, substituting it for one not in his field.

Where students are old enough to take the Type Indicator, as in 7th to 12th grades, their types can be ascertained, subject to confirmation by the students themselves. Teachers can then learn by direct observation how their subjects need to be presented in order to catch the interest of ST, SF, NF and NT types respectively, and can share their findings with other teachers. Feedback to the students about their types can add to their understanding of themselves and others, can reassure them that it is all right to be the kind of person they are, and can relieve the strain of personal conflicts at home or elsewhere by showing how these arise from differences in type. It can even help them to develop their perception and judgment. Page four of the *Introduction to Type* has instructions how to do it, exercising each kind of perception and each kind of judgment, separately, in turn, to find out what each can contribute to the solution of a problem.

Children in lower grades can also practice using the different kinds of perception and judgment one at a time in appropriate ways. Exact observation will exercise sensing. Figuring out possible ways to solve a difficulty will exercise intuition. Thinking out all the unintended consequences that may result from an action will exercise thinking. Weighing how other people will feel about things will exercise feeling.

An early clue to a child's type may be obtainable from his response to these activities. The sensing child should find the sensing exercise easier and more fun than the intuitive exercise. The little thinker will prefer thinking about consequences to guessing about other people's feelings. And so on. An observant teacher may be able to draw useful inferences as to the way each child's mind works and what will help him most. Whether she does or not, the children will benefit directly from practice in these four different, important ways of using their minds.

NEXT STEPS IN USING TYPE CONCEPTS

The Center for Applications of Psychological Type (1441 N. W. 6th Street, Suite B400, Gainesville, Florida 32601) is your best source for next steps. It can put you in touch with others who are using type concepts. The Center has contacts with people throughout the United States and in several other countries who can provide you with consulting help in applying type concepts to school situations. A comprehensive bibliography is available from the Center, and it has the most complete library of research and applied materials related to type.

ISTJ

Linear learner with strong need for order (SJ)
Likes direct experience (S)
Likes audio visuals (S); Lectures (I)
Enjoys working alone (I)
Likes well-defined goals (S)
Prefers practical tests (S)

ISFJ

Linear learner with strong need for order (SJ)
Likes listening to lectures (I)
Likes audio visuals (S)
Enjoys working alone (I)
Likes practical tests (S)

ISTP

Linear learner; needs help in organizing (SP)
Likes direct experience (S)
Likes lectures, audio visuals (S)
Enjoys working alone (I)

ISFP

Linear learner; needs help in organizing (SP)
Likes direct experience (S)
Needs well-defined goals (S)
Needs **harmony** in group projects (F)
Likes audio visuals, practical tests (S)
Enjoys working alone (I)

ESTP

Linear learner; needs help in organizing (SP)
Needs to know **why** before doing something (S)
Likes group projects, class reports, team competition (E)
Likes direct experience (S)
Likes audio visuals (S)
May like lecture (T)

ESFP

Linear learner; needs help in organizing (SP)
Likes direct experience (S)
Likes audio visuals; practical tests (S)
Needs to know **why** before doing something (S)
Likes group projects, team competition, class reports (E)
Needs orderly, well-defined goals (S)

ESTJ

Linear learner with strong need for structure (SJ)
Needs to know **why** before doing something (S)
Likes direct experience (S)
Likes group projects, class reports, team competition (E)
Likes audio visuals, practical tests (S)
May like lecture (T)

ESFJ

Linear learner with strong need for structure (SJ)
Needs to know **why** before doing something (S)
Needs well-defined goals (S)
Values **harmonious** group projects, team competition, class reports (E)
Likes audio visuals, practical tests (S)

INFJ

Can be global or linear (NJ)
Wants to consider theory first, then
  applications (N)
Enjoys working alone (I)
Prefers open-end instruction (N)
Needs **harmony** in group work (F)

INTJ

Can be global or linear (NJ)
Wants to consider theory first, then
  applications (N)
Enjoys working alone (I)
Prefers open-end instruction (N)
Good at paper-and-pencil tests (NT)

INFP

Global learner; needs sensitive
  instructor (NP)
Likes reading, listening (N)
Wants to consider theory first, then
  applications (N)
Needs **harmony** in group work (F)
Prefers open-end instruction (N)
Enjoys working alone (I)
Likes autonomy (NP)

INTP

Global learner, if with sensitive
  instructor (NP)
Likes reading, listening (N)
Wants to consider theory first, then
  applications (N)
Good at paper-and-pencil tests (NT)
Prefers open-end instruction (N)
Enjoys working alone (I)
Likes autonomy (NP)

ENFP

Global learner; needs sensitive
  instructor (NP)
Likes seminars (EN)
Likes reading if can settle down long
  enough (EN)
Likes **harmonious** group projects,
  team competition, class reports (EF)
Likes autonomy (NP)

ENTP

Global learner; needs sensitive
  instructor (NP)
Likes autonomy (NP)
Likes seminars (EN)
Likes reading, listening (N)
Wants to consider theory, then
  application (N)
Good at paper-and-pencil tests (NT)
Prefers open-end instruction (N)

ENFJ

Can be global or linear learner (NJ)
Likes seminars (EN)
Likes reading if can settle down long
  enough (ENF)
Likes **harmonious** group projects,
  class reports (EF)
Likes listening (N)
Likes pencil-and-paper tests (N)
Prefers open-end instruction (N)
Wants to consider theory, then
  applications (N)

ENTJ

Can be global or linear learner (NJ)
Likes seminars (EN)
Likes reading if can settle down long
  enough (ENF)
Likes group projects, class reports, team
  competition (E)
Likes listening (N)
Likes pencil-and-paper tests (N)
Prefers open-end instruction (N)
Wants to consider theory, then
  applications (N)

71

APPENDIX

INTRODUCTION TO TYPE

ISABEL BRIGGS MYERS

Published by
Center for Applications of Psychological Type, Inc.
1441 N. W. 6th Street—Suite B 400
Gainesville, Florida 32601

73

CONTENTS

FOREWORD

The questions in the Myers-Briggs Type Indicator are not important in themselves, but they do indicate basic preferences that have far-reaching effects. There is no right or wrong to these preferences. They simply produce different kinds of people who are interested in different things, are good in different fields and often find it hard to understand each other.

People with preferences opposite to yours tend to be opposite to you in many ways. They are likely to be weak where you are strong, and strong where you are weak. Each type has its own set of strengths and abilities.

An understanding of type in general and your own type in particular can help you choose your career. It can also help you deal with the problems and people in your life. The following pages provide a number of ways for you to explore your own preferences and verify your own type. The Indicator reports your type by four letters that show how you came out on each of the four preferences. You can check these letters against the explanations of the separate preferences (pages 2 and 6), the effects of the combinations of perception and judgment (page 3), the effects of the combinations of all four preferences in young people (pages 7-8), the adult descriptions (pages 9-16), and the effects of each preference in work situations (pages 17-18).

If the description of your reported type makes you feel comfortably understood, your four letters are probably right. If it does not fit you, one or more of the letters may be wrong. Sometimes people are not sure what they do prefer, or they disown their real preference for fear they ought to prefer the opposite, or their answers are affected by chance factors. If your reported type does not seem right to you, read the descriptions for the types that differ from it by a letter or two, and see which one comes closest to being a satisfactory description of yourself.

The Type Indicator is concerned with the valuable differences in people that result from the way they like to perceive and the way they like to judge. Succeeding at anything takes both perception and judgment. First you have to find out what the problem or situation is and what are the various things you might do about it. Then you have to decide which to do. Finding out is an exercise of perception. Deciding is an exercise of judgment. You have two basic ways of finding out and two basic ways of deciding.

Opposite ways of finding out: sensing and intuition. One way to find out is through your sensing (S). Your eyes and ears and other senses tell you what is actually there and actually happening. Sensing is especially useful for gathering the facts of a situation. The other way to find out is through your intuition (N) which shows you meanings and relationships and possibilities that are beyond the reach of your senses. Intuition is especially useful for seeing what you might do about a situation. You use both sensing and intuition, of course, but not both at once and not, in most cases, with equal liking.

If you like sensing better than intuition, you make more use of sensing, get to be more skillful with it, and grow expert at noticing all the observable facts. You tend to become realistic, practical, observant, fun-loving, and good at remembering a great number of facts and working with them.

If you like intuition better than sensing, you make more use of intuition, get to be more skillful with it, and grow expert at seeing a new possibility or solution. You tend to value imagination and inspirations, and to become good at new ideas, projects and problem-solving.

Opposite ways of deciding: thinking and feeling. One way to decide is through your thinking (T). Thinking predicts the logical result of any particular action you may take. Then it decides impersonally, on the basis of cause and effect. The other way to decide is through your feeling (F). Feeling takes into account anything that matters or is important to you or to other people (without requiring that it be logical), and decides on the basis of personal values. You use both thinking and feeling, of course, but not both at once and not, in most cases, with equal confidence.

If you trust thinking more than feeling and use it more, you grow to be most skillful in dealing with that part of the world which behaves logically (like machinery) with no unpredictable human reactions. You yourself tend to become logical, objective and consistent, and to make your decisions by analyzing and weighing the facts, including the unpleasant ones.

If you trust and use feeling more than thinking, you grow most skillful in dealing with people. You tend to become sympathetic, appreciative and tactful and to give great weight, when making any decisions, to the personal values that are involved, including those of other people.

The kind of perception you prefer to use, either sensing or intuition, can team up with whichever kind of judgment you prefer to use, either thinking or feeling. So there are four possible combinations, each producing a different set of characteristics—different interests, different values, different needs, different habits of mind and different surface traits.

Your own combination of perception and judgment makes a lot of difference in the kind of work you will do best and enjoy. If your daily work has most need for the kind of perception you naturally prefer, you will handle the job better and find it more satisfying. If your daily work has most need for the kind of deciding that comes naturally to you, your decisions will be better and will be made with more confidence. In choosing among careers, find out how much chance each will give you to use your own combination of perception and judgment.

3

EFFECTS OF THE COMBINATIONS OF
PERCEPTION AND JUDGMENT

Sensing plus Thinking. ST people are mainly interested in facts, since facts are what can be collected and verified directly by the senses—by seeing, hearing, touching, etc. And they make decisions on these facts by impersonal analysis, because the kind of judgment they trust is thinking, with its step-by-step process of reasoning from cause to effect, from premise to conclusion.

Sensing plus Feeling. SF people are also interested in facts, but make their decisions with personal warmth, because the kind of judgment they trust is feeling, with its power to weigh how much things matter to themselves and others.

Intuition plus Feeling. NF people make decisions with the same personal warmth. But, since they prefer intuition, their interest is not in facts but in possibilities, such as new projects, things that have not happened yet but might be made to happen, new truths that are not yet known but might be found out, or, above all, new possibilities for people.

Intuition plus Thinking. NT people share the interest in possibilities. But, since they prefer thinking, they approach these possibilities with impersonal analysis. Often the possibility they choose is a theoretical or technical one, with the human element more or less ignored.

The columns below present some of the results of these combinations.

	ST	SF	NF	NT
People who prefer:	SENSING + THINKING	SENSING + FEELING	INTUITION + FEELING	INTUITION + THINKING
focus their attention on:	Facts	Facts	Possibilities	Possibilities
and handle these with:	Impersonal analysis	Personal warmth	Personal warmth	Impersonal analysis
Thus they tend to become:	Practical and matter-of-fact	Sympathetic and friendly	Enthusiastic & insightful	Logical and ingenious
and find scope for their abilities in:	Technical skills with facts and objects	Practical help and services for people	Understanding & communicating with people	Theoretical and technical developments
for example:	Applied science Business Production Construction Etc.	Patient care Community service Sales Teaching Etc.	Behavioral science Research Literature & art Teaching Etc.	Physical science Research Management Forecasts & analysis Etc.

If you can tell which column comes closest to describing you, you can tell which two of the four processes (sensing, intuition, thinking and feeling) you naturally use most. One of those two will be your "favorite" process. The other is the "auxiliary" which supplies perception if the favorite is a judging process (T or F), or supplies judgment if the favorite is a perceptive process (S or N). Your greatest strengths come from the two you like, and it is important to trust and develop them. However, for some purposes, your less-liked kinds of perception and judgment will serve you much better—if you remember (and take the trouble) to use them.

MAKING FULL USE OF PERCEPTION AND JUDGMENT

To make full use of your perception and judgment, you need to use both kinds of perception and both kinds of judgment, each for the right purpose. This is a skill you can acquire by practice. Whenever you have a problem, a decision to make, a situation to deal with, try exercising each process by itself, consciously, purposefully, so that each can make its own contribution to the solution without interference from any other process. Start with your perceptive processes (S and N). Perception should always come before judgment.

1. Use your sensing for facing the facts, being realistic, finding exactly what the situation is, what you are doing, what other people are doing. Try to put aside all wishful thinking or sentiment that may blind you to the realities. Ask yourself how the situation would look to a wise, impartial bystander.

2. Use your intuition to discover all the possibilities—all the ways in which you might change the situation or your handling of it or other people's attitudes toward it. Try to put aside your natural assumption that you have been doing the one and only obviously right thing.

3. Use your thinking-judgment in an impersonal analysis of cause and effect. Include all the consequences of the alternative solutions, pleasant and unpleasant, those that weigh against the solution you prefer as well as those in its favor. Try to count the full cost of everything. Examine every misgiving you may have been suppressing out of loyalty to someone or liking for something or reluctance to change your stand.

4. Use your feeling-judgment to weigh just how deeply you care about the things that will be gained or lost by each of the alternative solutions. Make a fresh appraisal, trying not to let the temporary outweigh the permanent, however agreeable or disagreeable the immediate prospect may be. Consider also how the other people concerned will feel about the various outcomes, even if you think it unreasonable of them. And include their feelings and your own feelings along with the other facts, in deciding which solution will work out best.

You will probably choose, as usual, a solution that appeals to your favorite process, but on a sounder basis than usual because you will have considered facts, possibilities, consequences and human values. Ignoring any of these can lead to trouble. Intuitives may base a decision on some possibility without discovering the facts that will make it impossible. Sensing types may settle for a faulty solution to a problem because they assume no better one is possible. Thinking types may ignore human values and feeling types may ignore consequences.

You will find some steps in this exercise easier than others. The ones that use your best processes are rather fun. The others are harder, but worthwhile. If feeling is your favorite process, the attempt to see all the consequences of an act may show you that even the best intentions can go wrong unless thought through. If thinking is your favorite process, the attempt to learn how others feel about your plans may show why you meet so much opposition.

What makes the hard steps hard is that they call for the strengths of types opposite to yours. When your problem is important, you may be wise to consult someone to whom these strengths come naturally. It is startling to see how different a given situation can look to a person of opposite type, but it will help you to understand and use the neglected opposite side of yourself.

MUTUAL USEFULNESS OF OPPOSITE TYPES

The clearest vision of the future comes only from an intuitive, the most practical realism only from a sensing type, the most incisive analysis only from a thinker, and the most skillful handling of people only from a feeling type. Success for any enterprise demands a variety of types, each in the right place.

Opposite types can supplement each other in any joint undertaking. When two people approach a problem from opposite sides, each sees things not visible to the other. Unfortunately, they seldom see each other's point of view. Too much oppositeness makes it hard for people to work well together. The best teamwork is usually done by people who differ on one or two preferences only. This much difference is useful, and the two or three preferences they have in common help them to understand each other and communicate.

When extreme opposites must work or live together, an understanding of type does much to lessen the friction. Disagreement is less irritating when Smith recognizes that it would hardly be normal for Jones to agree. Jones is not being willfully contrary. He is simply being an opposite type, and opposite types can be tremendously useful to each other when given the chance. The lists below show some of the specific ways.

INTUITIVE NEEDS A SENSING TYPE:	SENSING TYPE NEEDS AN INTUITIVE:
To bring up pertinent facts	To bring up new possibilities
To apply experience to problems	To supply ingenuity on problems
To read the fine print in a contract	To read the signs of coming change
To notice what needs attention now	To see how to prepare for the future
To have patience	To have enthusiasm
To keep track of essential detail	To watch for new essentials
To face difficulties with realism	To tackle difficulties with zest
To remind that the joys of the present are important	To show that the joys of the future are worth working for

FEELING TYPE NEEDS A THINKER:	THINKER NEEDS A FEELING TYPE:
To analyze	To persuade
To organize	To conciliate
To find the flaws in advance	To forecast how others will feel
To reform what needs reforming	To arouse enthusiasm
To hold consistently to a policy	To teach
To weigh "the law and the evidence"	To sell
To fire people when necessary	To advertise
To stand firm against opposition	To appreciate the thinker

A-5

REMAINING PREFERENCES AND SUMMARY

Outer world or inner world: E or I. Your main fields of interest are apt to be directly related to the kind of perception and kind of judgment you prefer, that is, to your SN and TF preferences. But the sort of work you will most enjoy doing within those fields may depend on your EI preference,—whether you like to use your favorite process extravertedly (E) in the outer world of people and things, or introvertedly (I) in the inner world of concepts and ideas.

Take the ST people for example. The introverts among them (IST) like to organize facts and principles related to a situation, which is the useful thing to do in economics or law. The extraverts among them (EST) like to organize the situation itself (including any idle bystanders) and get it moving, which is the useful thing to do in business or industry.

Jung, who invented the terms, looked upon extraversion and introversion as valuable opposites, which everyone uses but not with equal ease. Extraverts tend to be more interested and comfortable when they are working actively with people or things. Introverts tend to be more interested and comfortable when their work involves ideas and requires a good deal of their activity to take place quietly inside their heads.

Judging attitude or perceptive attitude toward the outer world: J or P. The final preference, JP, is between the use of perception and the use of judgment in dealing with the outer world. The J people rely mainly on a judging process for this purpose (thinking or feeling, whichever they prefer), and live in a planned, decided, orderly way, wanting to regulate life and control it. The P people rely mainly on a perceptive process (sensing or intuition) for dealing with the outer world, and live in a flexible, spontaneous way, wanting to understand life and adapt to it.

This JP preference works differently with extraverts and introverts. With extraverts the favorite process is, by definition, the one they prefer to use in the outer world. Therefore the extraverts' favorite process governs their JP preference. Extraverts whose favorite process is a judging one come out J. Extraverts whose favorite process is a perceptive one come out P.

With introverts the favorite process is, by definition, the one they prefer to use in the inner world. They do their extraverting mostly with their auxiliary. Their auxiliary process, therefore, is what governs their JP preference. Introverts whose favorite process is a judging one come out P because their auxiliary is perceptive. And introverts whose favorite process is a perceptive one come out J.

Summary of the four preferences.
Your type is the result of your own combination of preferences, which can be stated for convenience in four letters. For example, ISTJ means an introvert liking sensing and thinking and a mainly judging attitude toward the outer world. ENFP means an extravert liking intuition and feeling and a mainly perceptive attitude toward the outer world. (N is used for intuition because I stands for introversion.) The Type Table on the back cover shows the favorite and auxiliary processes for each of the sixteen types. Brief sketches are given on pp. 7-8, longer descriptions on pp. 9-16.

EI Preference	
Extraversion	Introversion

SN Preference	
Sensing	Intuition

TF Preference	
Thinking	Feeling

JP Preference	
Judgment	Perception

EFFECTS OF THE COMBINATIONS OF ALL

SENSING TYPES

WITH THINKING	WITH FEELING
ISTJ Serious, quiet, earn success by concentration and thoroughness. Practical, orderly, matter-of-fact, logical, realistic and dependable. See to it that everything is well organized. Take responsibility. Make up their own minds as to what should be accomplished and work toward it steadily, regardless of protests or distractions. Live their outer life more with thinking, inner more with sensing.	**ISFJ** Quiet, friendly, responsible and conscientious. Work devotedly to meet their obligations and serve their friends and school. Thorough, painstaking, accurate. May need time to master technical subjects, as their interests are not often technical. Patient with detail and routine. Loyal, considerate, concerned with how other people feel. Live their outer life more with feeling, inner more with sensing.
ISTP Cool onlookers, quiet, reserved, observing and analyzing life with detached curiosity and unexpected flashes of original humor. Usually interested in impersonal principles, cause and effect, or how and why mechanical things work. Exert themselves no more than they think necessary, because any waste of energy would be inefficient. Live their outer life more with sensing, inner more with thinking.	**ISFP** Retiring, quietly friendly, sensitive, modest about their abilities. Shun disagreements, do not force their opinions or values on others. Usually do not care to lead but are often loyal followers. May be rather relaxed about assignments or getting things done, because they enjoy the present moment and do not want to spoil it by undue haste or exertion. Live their outer life more with sensing, inner more with feeling.
ESTP Matter-of-fact, do not worry or hurry, enjoy whatever comes along. Tend to like mechanical things and sports, with friends on the side. May be a bit blunt or insensitive. Can do math or science when they see the need. Dislike long explanations. Are best with real things that can be worked, handled, taken apart or put back together. Live their outer life more with sensing, inner more with thinking.	**ESFP** Outgoing, easygoing, accepting, friendly, fond of a good time. Like sports and making things. Know what's going on and join in eagerly. Find remembering facts easier than mastering theories. Are best in situations that need sound common sense and practical ability with people as well as with things. Live their outer life more with sensing, inner more with feeling.
ESTJ Practical realists, matter-of-fact, with a natural head for business or mechanics. Not interested in subjects they see no use for, but can apply themselves when necessary. Like to organize and run activities. Tend to run things well, especially if they remember to consider other people's feelings and points of view when making their decisions. Live their outer life more with thinking, inner more with sensing.	**ESFJ** Warm-hearted, talkative, popular, conscientious, born cooperators, active committee members. Always doing something nice for someone. Work best with plenty of encouragement and praise. Little interest in abstract thinking or technical subjects. Main interest is in things that directly and visibly affect people's lives. Live their outer life more with feeling, inner more with sensing.

INTROVERTS — JUDGING / PERCEPTIVE

EXTRAVERTS — PERCEPTIVE / JUDGING

A-7

INTUITIVES

WITH FEELING   WITH THINKING

INFJ	INTJ
Succeed by perseverance, originality and desire to do whatever is needed or wanted. Put their best efforts into their work. Quietly forceful, conscientious, concerned for others. Respected for their firm principles. Likely to be honored and followed for their clear convictions as to how best to serve the common good. Live their outer life more with feeling, inner more with intuition.	Have original minds and great drive which they use only for their own purposes. In fields that appeal to them they have a fine power to organize a job and carry it through with or without help. Skeptical, critical, independent, determined, often stubborn. Must learn to yield less important points in order to win the most important. Live their outer life more with thinking, inner more with intuition.
INFP	**INTP**
Full of enthusiasms and loyalties, but seldom talk of these until they know you well. Care about learning, ideas, language, and independent projects of their own. Apt to be on yearbook staff, perhaps as editor. Tend to undertake too much, then somehow get it done. Friendly, but often too absorbed in what they are doing to be sociable or notice much. Live their outer life more with intuition, inner more with feeling.	Quiet, reserved, brilliant in exams, especially in theoretical or scientific subjects. Logical to the point of hair-splitting. Interested mainly in ideas, with little liking for parties or small talk. Tend to have very sharply defined interests. Need to choose careers where some strong interest of theirs can be used and useful. Live their outer life more with intuition, inner more with thinking.
ENFP	**ENTP**
Warmly enthusiastic, high-spirited, ingenious, imaginative. Able to do almost anything that interests them. Quick with a solution for any difficulty and ready to help anyone with a problem. Often rely on their ability to improvise instead of preparing in advance. Can always find compelling reasons for whatever they want. Live their outer life more with intuition, inner more with feeling.	Quick, ingenious, good at many things. Stimulating company, alert and outspoken, argue for fun on either side of a question. Resourceful in solving new and challenging problems, but may neglect routine assignments. Turn to one new interest after another. Can always find logical reasons for whatever they want. Live their outer life more with intuition, inner more with thinking.
ENFJ	**ENTJ**
Responsive and responsible. Feel real concern for what others think and want, and try to handle things with due regard for other people's feelings. Can present a proposal or lead a group discussion with ease and tact. Sociable, popular, active in school affairs, but put time enough on their studies to do good work. Live their outer life more with feeling, inner more with intuition.	Hearty, frank, able in studies, leaders in activities. Usually good in anything that requires reasoning and intelligent talk, such as public speaking. Are well-informed and keep adding to their fund of knowledge. May sometimes be more positive and confident than their experience in an area warrants. Live their outer life more with thinking, inner more with intuition.

JUDGING   INTROVERTS   PERCEPTIVE

PERCEPTIVE   EXTRAVERTS   JUDGING

EXTRAVERTED THINKING TYPES
ESTJ and ENTJ

Extraverted thinkers use their thinking to run as much of the world as may be theirs to run. They organize their facts and operations well in advance, define their objectives and make a systematic drive to reach these objectives on schedule. Through reliance on thinking, they become logical, analytical, often critical, impersonal and unlikely to be convinced by anything but reasoning.

They enjoy being executives, deciding what ought to be done, and giving the necessary orders. They have little patience with confusion, inefficiency, halfway measures, or anything aimless and ineffective, and they know how to be tough when the situation calls for toughness.

They think conduct should be governed by logic, and govern their own that way as much as they can. They live according to a definite formula that embodies their basic judgments about the world. Any change in their ways requires a deliberate change in the formula.

Like other judging types, they run some risk of neglecting perception. They need to stop and listen to the other person's side of the matter, especially with people who are not in a position to talk back. They seldom find this easy, but if (repeat, if) they do not manage to do it, they may judge too hastily, without enough facts or enough regard for what other people think or feel.

Feeling is their least developed process. If they suppress or neglect it too long, it can explode in damaging ways. They need to make some conscious use of feeling, preferably in appreciation of other people's merits,—an art that comes less naturally to thinkers than to feeling types. Thinkers can, if they will, "make it a rule" in their formula to mention what is well done, not merely what needs correcting. The results will be worthwhile, both in their work and in their private lives.

ESTJ
With sensing as auxiliary

Look at things with their sensing rather than their intuition. Hence are most interested in realities perceived by their five senses, which makes them matter-of-fact, practical, realistic, factually-minded, concerned with here and now. More curious about new things than new ideas. Want ideas, plans and decisions to be based on solid fact.

Solve problems by expertly applying and adapting past experience.

Like work where they can achieve immediate, visible and tangible results. Have a natural bent for business and industry, production and construction. Enjoy administration and getting things organized and done. Do not listen to their own intuition very much, so tend to need an intuitive around to sell them on the value of new ideas.

ENTJ
With intuition as auxiliary

Look at things with their intuition rather than their sensing, hence are mainly interested in seeing the possibilities beyond what is present or obvious or known. Intuition heightens their intellectual interest, curiosity for new ideas, tolerance for theory, taste for complex problems, insight, vision and concern for long range possibilities and consequences.

Are seldom content in jobs that make no demand on intuition. Need problems to solve and are expert at finding new solutions. Interest is in the broad picture, not in detailed procedures or facts. Tend to choose like-minded intuitives as associates. Also tend to need someone with sensing around to keep them from overlooking relevant facts and important details.

A-9

INTROVERTED THINKING TYPES
ISTP and INTP

Introverted thinkers use their thinking to analyze the world, not to run it. They organize ideas and facts, not situations or people unless they must. Relying on thinking makes them logical, impersonal, objectively critical, not likely to be convinced by anything but reasoning. Being introverts, they focus their thinking on the principles underlying things rather than on the things themselves. Since it is hard to switch their thinking from ideas to details of daily living, they lead their outer lives mainly with their preferred perceptive process, S or N. They are quiet, reserved, detachedly curious and quite adaptable—till one of their ruling principles is violated, at which point they stop adapting.

If (repeat, if) they do not develop their perception, they will have too little knowledge or experience of the world. Their thinking will have no real relationship to the problems of their time, and not very much will come of it.

In the field of ideas they are decisive, though socially they may be rather shy except with their best friends. Their special problem is to make their ideas understood. Wanting to state exact truth, they tend to state it in a way too complicated for most people to follow. If they will use simple statements, even if they think the point is too obvious to be worth making, their ideas will be much more widely understood and accepted.

Feeling is their least developed process. They are not apt to know, unless told, what matters emotionally to another person, but they can and should act on the principle that people do care about having their merits appreciated and their point of view respectfully considered. Both the working life and the personal life of the introverted thinker will go better if they take the trouble to do two simple things—say an appreciative word when praise is honestly due, and mention the points where they agree with another person before they bring up the points where they disagree.

ISTP
With sensing as auxiliary

See the realities. Great capacity for facts and details. Good at applied science and at mechanics and the properties of materials and things. With nontechnical interests, can use general principles to bring order out of masses of confused data and meaning out of unorganized facts. May be analysts of markets, sales, securities or statistics of any kind.

Likely to be patient, accurate, good with their hands, fond of sports and outdoors, and have a gift of fun.

Great believers in economy of effort, which is an asset if they judge accurately how much effort is needed, and do efficiently what the situation demands. If not, economy of effort can become mere laziness and little will get done.

INTP
With intuition as auxiliary

See the possibilities. Value facts mainly in relation to theory. Good at pure science, research, math, and the more complicated engineering problems. With nontechnical interests, make scholars, teachers, abstract thinkers in economics, philosophy, psychology, etc.

Apt to have insight, ingenuity, quick understanding, intellectual curiosity, fertility of ideas about problems. More interested in reaching solutions than in putting them into practice, which others can do as well.

Need to check out even their most attractive intuitive projects against the facts and the limitations these impose. Otherwise may squander their energies in pursuing impossibilities.

EXTRAVERTED FEELING TYPES
ESFJ and ENFJ

Extraverted feeling types radiate warmth and fellowship. Reliance on feeling gives them a very personal approach to life, since feeling judges everything by a set of personal values. Being extraverts, they focus their feeling on the people around them, placing a very high value on harmonious human contacts. They are friendly, tactful, sympathetic, and can almost always express the right feeling.

They are particularly warmed by approval and sensitive to indifference. Much of their pleasure and satisfaction comes not only from others' warmth of feeling but from their own; they enjoy admiring people and so tend to concentrate on a person's most admirable qualities. They try to live up to their ideals and are loyal to respected persons, institutions and causes.

They are unusually able to see value in other people's opinions. And even when the opinions are conflicting, they have faith that harmony can somehow be achieved and often manage to bring it about. Their intense concentration on other people's viewpoints sometimes makes them lose sight of the value of their own. They are best at jobs that deal with people and any situation where the needed cooperation can be won by good will. They think best when talking with people and enjoy talk. It takes special effort for them to be brief and businesslike.

Being judging types, they like to have matters settled and decided, but they do not need or want to make all the decisions themselves. They have many "shoulds" and "should nots" and may express these freely. They are conscientious, persevering, orderly even in small matters, and inclined to expect others to be the same.

If (repeat _if_) they do not develop their perception, they will, with the best of intentions, act on assumptions that turn out to be wrong. They are especially likely to be blind to the facts when there is a situation that is disagreeable or a criticism that hurts. It is harder for them than for other types to see things they wish were not true. If they fail to face disagreeable facts, they will sweep their problems under the rug instead of finding good solutions.

ESFJ
With sensing as auxiliary

Look at things with their sensing, which makes them practical, realistic, matter-of-fact, concerned with here and now. Appreciate and enjoy their material possessions and details of direct experience. Like to base plans and decisions upon known facts.

Enjoy variety, but usually adapt excellently to routine.

Compassion and awareness of physical conditions often attract them to nursing (where they provide warmth and comfort as well as devoted care) and to health professions in general.

ENFJ
With intuition as auxiliary

Look at things with their intuition rather than their sensing, hence are mainly interested in seeing the possibilities beyond what is present or obvious or known. Intuition heightens their understanding, long-range vision, insight, curiosity about new ideas, love of books and tolerance for theory.

Likely to have a gift of expression, but may use it in speaking to audiences rather than in writing. Interest in possibilities for people attracts them often to counseling in the fields of career choice or personal development.

Introverted feeling types have a wealth of warmth and enthusiasm, but may not show it till they know you well. Reliance on feeling leads them to judge everything by personal values; being introverts, they choose these values without reference to the judgment of others. They know what is most important to them and protect it at all costs. Loyalties and ideals govern their lives. Their deepest feelings are seldom expressed, since their tenderness and passionate conviction are masked by their quiet reserve.

Their feeling being introverted, they conduct their outer lives mainly with their preferred perceptive process, either sensing or intuition. This makes them open-minded, flexible and adaptable—until one of the things they value most deeply seems in danger—at which point they stop adapting. Except for the sake of their work they have little wish to impress or dominate. The friends who mean most to them are the people who understand their values and the goals they are working toward.

They are twice as good when working at a job they believe in; their feeling puts added energy behind their efforts. They want their work to contribute to something that matters to them—human understanding or happiness or health, or perhaps to the perfecting of some project or undertaking. They want to have a purpose beyond their paycheck, no matter how big the check. They are perfectionists wherever their feeling is engaged and are usually happiest at some individual work involving their personal values.

Being idealists, they measure their accomplishments against an inner standard of perfection, instead of what is actually possible. They may suffer from too great self-demand, feeling that the contrast between their inner ideal and outer reality is somehow their fault. They need to find something they really care about, and then work to achieve it. With an ideal to work for, and good development of perception to help them recognize realistic difficulties and possible solutions, they can achieve a high degree of self-confident drive.

If (repeat if) they do not find a way to use their energies in the service of an ideal, they tend to become oversensitive and vulnerable, losing confidence in life and in themselves. If their perception is undeveloped, they may have so little realism that they aspire to the impossible and achieve frustratingly little.

ISFP
With sensing as auxiliary

See the realities. Mildly resemble ESFP, especially in seeing and meeting the need of the moment. Can pay close, unbroken attention for long periods, when work requires monitoring or close observation.

Show their warmth more by deeds than words. Compassionate toward all helpless creatures. Work well at jobs requiring devotion. Gentle, considerate, retiring. Consistently underestimate and understate themselves. May find satisfactory outlets in fields where taste, discrimination and a sense of beauty are of value.

INFP
With intuition as auxiliary

See the possibilities. Mildly resemble ENFP, especially in liking to concentrate on projects and disliking details not related to a deep interest. Understanding, tend to have insight and long-range vision. Curious about new ideas, fond of books and language. Apt to have skill in expressing themselves.

Ingenious and persuasive on the subject of their enthusiasms. Especially interested in possibilities for people. Enjoy counseling and teaching. With high ability, may excel in literature, art, science or psychology.

EXTRAVERTED SENSING TYPES

ESTP and ESFP

Extraverted sensing makes the adaptable realists, who good-naturedly accept and use the facts around them, whatever these are. They know what the facts are, since they notice and remember more than any other type. They know what goes on, who wants what and who doesn't. And they do not fight those facts. There is a sort of effortless economy in the way they deal with a situation, never taking the hard way when an easier one will work.

Often they can get other people to adapt, too. Being perceptive types, they look for the satisfying solution, instead of trying to impose any "should" or "must" of their own, and people generally like them well enough to consider any compromise that they suggest "might work". They are unprejudiced, open-minded, and usually patient, easygoing and tolerant of everyone—including themselves. They enjoy life. They don't get wrought up. Thus they may be very good at easing tense situations and pulling conflicting factions together.

Their expert sensing may show itself: (a) in a gift for machinery and the handling of tools and materials for craft or artistic purposes, or in ability to recognize quality, line, color, texture or detail; (b) in a capacity for exact facts, even when separate and unrelated, and the ability to absorb, remember and apply them; (c) in a continuous awareness, an ability to see the need of the moment and turn easily to meet it.

They are strong in the art of living, appreciate and enjoy their material possessions, and take the time to acquire and care for these. They value enjoyment, from good food and good clothes to music, art and all the products of the amusement industry. Even without these helps, they get fun out of life, which makes them fun to be with.

Being realists, they get more from first-hand experience than from study, are more effective on the job than on written tests, and doubly effective when on familiar ground. Seeing the value of new ideas, theories and possibilities may well come a bit hard, because intuition is their least developed process.

Their net effectiveness depends on whether they develop their judgment to the point where it can balance their easygoing sensing and give some direction to their lives. If (repeat, if) their judgment is not good enough to give them any character or stick-to-it-iveness, they may adapt mainly to their own love of a good time, and become lazy, unstable and generally shallow.

ESTP With thinking as auxiliary	ESFP With feeling as auxiliary
Like to make decisions with their thinking rather than their feeling. Hence are more aware of the logical consequences of an act or decision. Thinking gives them more grasp of underlying principles, helps with math and theory and makes it easier for them to get tough when the situation calls for toughness.	Like to make decisions with their feeling rather than their thinking. Feeling gives them tact, sympathy, interest in people, ease in handling human contacts, and may make them too easy as disciplinarians. Feeling also makes for artistic taste and judgment, but is no help with analysis.

ISTJ and ISFJ

Introverted sensing types are made particularly dependable by their combination of preferences. They use their favorite process, sensing, in their inner life, and base their ideas on a deep, solid accumulation of stored impressions, which gives them some pretty unshakable ideas. Then they use their preferred kind of judgment, thinking or feeling, to run their outer life. Thus they have a complete, realistic, practical respect both for the facts and for whatever responsibilities these facts create. Sensing provides the facts. And after the introvert's characteristic pause for reflection, their judgment accepts the responsibilities.

They can remember and use any number of facts, but want them all accurate. They like everything kept factual, clearly stated, not too complex. Not till you know them very well do you discover that behind their outer calm they are seeing the facts from an intensely individual, often delightfully humorous angle. Their private reaction, the way a thing will strike them, is quite unpredictable.

But what they actually do about it will be sound and sensible because what they do is part of their outer life and so is governed by their best judgment. No type is more thorough, painstaking, systematic, hard-working, or patient with detail and routine. Their perseverance tends to stabilize everything with which they are connected. They do not enter into things impulsively, but once in, they are very hard to distract, discourage or stop. They do not quit unless experience convinces them they are wrong.

As administrators, their practical judgment and memory for detail make them conservative, consistent, able to cite cases to support their evaluations of people and methods. They will go to any amount of trouble if they "can see the need of it," but hate to be required to do anything that "doesn't make sense." Usually it is hard for them to see any sense in needs that differ widely from their own. But once they are convinced that a given thing does matter a lot to a given person, the need becomes a fact to be respected and they may go to generous lengths to help satisfy it, while still holding that it doesn't make sense.

Their effectiveness depends on their developing adequate judgment for dealing with the world. If (repeat, if) judgment remains childish, the world is not dealt with, the person retreats into silent preoccupation with inner reactions to sense-impressions, and not much of value is likely to result.

ISTJ With thinking as auxiliary	ISFJ With feeling as auxiliary
Mildly resemble the extraverted thinking types. Thinking stresses analysis, logic and decisiveness. In their personal relationships, they may need to take extra pains to understand and appreciate. They will then be in no danger of overriding people less forceful than they are, and will find themselves richly repaid both in their work and in their private lives.	Mildly resemble the extraverted feeling types. Feeling stresses loyalty, consideration and the common welfare. They are sympathetic, tactful, kind and genuinely concerned, which traits make them very supportive to persons in need of support. They are often attracted to fields where systematic attention to detail is combined with a care for people, as in the health professions.

EXTRAVERTED INTUITIVE TYPES

ENTP and ENFP

The extraverted intuitives are the enthusiastic innovators. They are always seeing new possibilities—new ways of doing things, or quite new and fascinating things that might be done—and they go all out in pursuit of these. They have a lot of imagination and initiative for originating projects, and a lot of impulsive energy for carrying them out. They are wholly confident of the worth of their inspirations, tireless with the problems involved, and ingenious with the difficulties. They get so interested in the current project that they think of little else.

They get other people interested too. Being perceptive types, they try to understand people rather than to judge them; often, by putting their minds to it, they achieve an uncanny knowledge of what makes a given person tick, and use this to win support for their project. They adapt to other people in the way they present their objective, but never to the point of giving it up. Their faith in their intuition makes them too independent and individualistic to be conformists, but they keep a lively circle of contacts as a consequence of their versatility and their easy interest in almost everything.

In their quieter moments, their auxiliary gives them some balancing introversion and adds depth to the insights supplied by their intuition. At its best, their insight, tempered by judgment, may amount to wisdom.

Their trouble is that they hate uninspired routine and find it remarkably hard to apply themselves to humdrum detail unconnected with any major interest. Worse yet, even their projects begin to seem routine and lose attraction as soon as the main problems are solved and the rest seems clear sailing. They may discipline themselves to carry through, but they are happiest and most effective in jobs that permit of one project after another, with someone else taking over as soon as the situation is well in hand.

If their judgment and self-discipline are not developed, they will throw themselves into ill-chosen projects, leave them unfinished, and squander their inspirations, abilities and energies on unimportant, half-done jobs. At their worst, they will be unstable, undependable, fickle and easily discouraged.

ENTP With thinking as auxiliary	ENFP With feeling as auxiliary
More independent, analytical and critical of their inspirations, more impersonal in their relations with people, more apt to consider only how others may affect their projects and not how the projects may affect others. May be inventors, scientists, troubleshooters, promoters, or almost anything that it interests them to be.	More enthusiastic, more concerned with people and skillful in handling them. Much drawn to counseling, where each new person presents a fresh problem to be solved and fresh possibilities to be communicated. May be inspired and inspiring teachers, scientists, artists, advertising or sales people, or almost anything that it interests them to be.

INTJ and INFJ

The introverted intuitives are the great innovators in the field of ideas. They trust their intuitive insights as to the relationships and meanings of things, regardless of established authority or popular beliefs. They trust their vision of the possibilities, regardless of universal skepticism. And they want to see their ideas worked out in practice, accepted and applied.

Consequently, they have to deal firmly with the outer world, which they do by means of their preferred kind of judgment, either T or F. Thus they back up their original insight with the determination, perseverance and enduring purpose of the judging types. When they are driving to turn an inspiration into a reality, problems stimulate rather than discourage them. The impossible takes a little longer—but not much.

Certain dangers arise from their single-minded concentration. They see their goal so clearly that they may not even look for the other things they need to see—the things that conflict with their goal. They may not take the trouble to learn the details of the situation they propose to change. Since sensing is their least developed process, they can easily overlook relevant facts and the limitations these facts impose.

They may not consider the opposition they will meet, its strength or source or probable grounds. They may not consider the possibility that something is wrong with their idea. In scientific research or engineering design, a trial of their boldly ingenious ideas will visibly succeed—or fail and show where the idea has to be revised. They need to be particularly alert for flaws in their ideas in those fields where their insights cannot be tested so clearly.

Their auxiliary process, if adequately developed, can supply needed criticism of their ideas. Judgment can be used to foresee difficulties and decide what needs to be done about them. Most original inspirations need to be modified in the light of facts. Ideas need to be worked out and perfected to lessen objections. The best ideas still need to be presented to the world in terms understandable to other types.

If (repeat, if) their judgment is not developed, they cannot criticize their own inner vision, and they tend to reject all judgments from outside. As a result, they cannot shape their inspirations into effective action. Their ideas will go to waste, and they may be regarded only as visionaries or cranks.

INTJ
With thinking as auxiliary

Most individualistic and most independent of all the types.

Resemble extraverted thinkers in organizing ability and a tendency to ignore the views and feelings of those who don't agree with them.

Logical, critical, decisive, determined, often stubborn.

Tend to drive others almost as hard as they drive themselves.

Apt to be effective, relentless reorganizers. Can be efficient executives, rich in ideas.

INFJ
With feeling as auxiliary

Less obviously individualistic, more apt to win cooperation than to demand it.

Resemble extraverted feeling types in their sympathetic handling of people and in a tendency to ignore harsh and uncongenial facts.

May apply their ingenuity to problems of human welfare on their own and in their own way.

Can be successful executives, especially where affairs can be conducted on a personal basis.

INTROVERTS	EXTRAVERTS
Like quiet for concentration.	Like variety and action.
Tend to be careful with details, dislike sweeping statements.	Tend to be faster, dislike complicated procedures.
Have trouble remembering names and faces.	Are often good at greeting people.
Tend not to mind working on one project for a long time uninterruptedly.	Are often impatient with long slow jobs.
Are interested in the idea behind their job.	Are interested in the results of their job, in getting it done and in how other people do it.
Dislike telephone intrusions and interruptions.	Often don't mind the interruption of answering the telephone.
Like to think a lot before they act, sometimes without acting.	Often act quickly, sometimes without thinking.
Work contentedly alone.	Like to have people around.
Have some problems communicating.	Usually communicate freely.

FEELING TYPES	THINKING TYPES
Tend to be very aware of other people and their feelings.	Are relatively unemotional and uninterested in people's feelings.
Enjoy pleasing people, even in unimportant things.	May hurt people's feelings without knowing it.
Like harmony. Efficiency may be badly disturbed by office feuds.	Like analysis and putting things into logical order. Can get along without harmony.
Often let decisions be influenced by their own or other people's personal likes and wishes.	Tend to decide impersonally, sometimes ignoring people's wishes.
Need occasional praise.	Need to be treated fairly.
Dislike telling people unpleasant things.	Are able to reprimand people or fire them when necessary.
Relate well to most people.	Tend to relate well only to other thinking types.
Tend to be sympathetic.	May seem hard-hearted.

INTUITIVE TYPES

Like solving new problems.

Dislike doing the same thing over and over again.

Enjoy learning a new skill more than using it.

Work in bursts of energy powered by enthusiasm, with slack periods in between.

Put two and two together quickly.

Are impatient with routine details.

Are patient with complicated situations.

Follow their inspirations, good or bad.

Often get their facts a bit wrong.

Dislike taking time for precision.

SENSING TYPES

Dislike new problems unless there are standard ways to solve them.

Like an established way of doing things.

Enjoy using skills already learned more than learning new ones.

Work more steadily, with realistic idea of how long it will take.

Usually reach a conclusion step by step.

Are patient with routine details.

Are impatient when the details get complicated.

Don't often get inspired, and rarely trust the inspiration when they do.

Seldom make errors of fact.

Tend to be good at precise work.

PERCEPTIVE TYPES

Tend to be good at adapting to changing situations.

Don't mind leaving things open for alterations.

May have trouble making decisions.

May start too many projects and have difficulty in finishing them.

May postpone unpleasant jobs.

Want to know all about a new job.

Tend to be curious and welcome new light on a thing, situation or person.

JUDGING TYPES

Best when they can plan their work and follow the plan.

Like to get things settled and wrapped up.

May decide things too quickly.

May dislike to interrupt the project they are on for a more urgent one.

May not notice new things that need to be done.

Want only the essentials needed to get on with it.

Tend to be satisfied once they reach a judgment on a thing, situation or person.

TYPE TABLE

INTUITIVES

WITH THINKING

INTJ Introverted Intuition with thinking	**INTP** Introverted Thinking with intuition

WITH FEELING

INFJ Introverted Intuition with feeling	**INFP** Introverted Feeling with intuition

ENTP
Extraverted Intuition
with thinking

ENTJ
Extraverted Thinking
with intuition

ENFP
Extraverted Intuition
with feeling

ENFJ
Extraverted Feeling
with intuition

SENSING TYPES

WITH FEELING

ISFJ Introverted Sensing with feeling	**ISFP** Introverted Feeling with sensing

WITH THINKING

ISTJ Introverted Sensing with thinking	**ISTP** Introverted Thinking with sensing

ESFP
Extraverted Sensing
with feeling

ESFJ
Extraverted Feeling
with sensing

ESTP
Extraverted Sensing
with thinking

ESTJ
Extraverted Thinking
with sensing

JUDGING   PERCEPTIVE   PERCEPTIVE   JUDGING
INTROVERTS   EXTRAVERTS